# THE HIDDEN FORCE

# THE
# HIDDEN FORCE

A REPORT OF THE
INTERNATIONAL CONFERENCE
ON MIDDLE LEVEL MANPOWER,
SAN JUAN, PUERTO RICO,
OCTOBER 10-12, 1962

**Francis W. Godwin**
Consultant, Overseas Economic Development

**Richard N. Goodwin**
Secretary General, International Peace Corps Secretariat

**William F. Haddad**
Associate Director, U.S. Peace Corps

*Foreword by Sargent Shriver*

HARPER & ROW, PUBLISHERS
NEW YORK, EVANSTON, AND LONDON

# Contents

# ACKNOWLEDGMENT

To condense the great mass of discussions, speeches, proceedings and technical papers of the San Juan Conference into a digest of this size would not have been possible in any reasonable time without very capable collaboration and assistance. For their help in extracting and organizing the material, in preparing drafts of certain sections, and in furnishing suggestions and criticism a real debt of gratitude is owed to Philip Cook, Richard Elwell and Paul Vanderwood of the U.S. Peace Corps Evaluation Staff; to Dan H. Fenn, Staff Assistant to the President; to David Swit of the San Juan Conference press staff; and to Frank Prial of the Newark *News*.

## STATEMENTS

Not only is this Conference one of the largest ever held on any aspect of economic development, it is also one of the most significant. You will consider the means of establishing the human base on which economic and social development must rest.

I am particularly gratified that these international deliberations have been sponsored by the United States Peace Corps. The Peace Corps represents in a clear and dramatic way the desire of American men and women to share in the task of improving the welfare of the world's people. They have shown a dedication to service in the Peace Corps which transcends national boundaries and policies to strike the common chord of hope for all humanity.

> JOHN F. KENNEDY
> *Message to the delegates,*
> *International Conference*
> *on Middle Level Manpower,*
> *October 1962*

We came here to talk about the development of human skills—the enhancement of the technical capacity of men and women. But the larger implication is that we are discussing the enrichments of life—and thereby the emergence of a true sense of community within nations and on the world scene.

Our true goal is the day when every individual will have the opportunity—and the means to use the opportunity—to participate fully and effectively in the promising life that twentieth-century technology is opening before us.

> LYNDON B. JOHNSON
> *Opening Remarks, International*
> *Conference on Middle Level Manpower,*
> *October 1962*

# Foreword

by Sargent Shriver,

Director, U.S. Peace Corps

This book is the record of a significant meeting in the history of postwar economic development—a meeting which brought together much of the best of past thought and achievement to point the way to future programs for increasing the welfare of man.

Last October, forty-three nations and several international organizations met in Puerto Rico for three days to discuss the urgent need for skilled men and women by countries searching for a road to rapid progress. Initially, the Peace Corps had conceived of this conference as a forum to discuss the role of volunteers in emerging countries. Attendance was to be restricted to those countries participating in Peace Corps programs as of April 1, 1962. But it soon became apparent that the Puerto Rico Conference was a historic opportunity to attack the entire problem of the need for skilled manpower and to seek solutions for this problem. The industrialized nations of Western Europe, Japan, New Zealand, and Australia—those countries which had the resources and skills to help others—asked to come and were invited. International organizations became interested; and the United Nations, the ILO, the OECD, and others were asked to participate. Soon, the Peace Corps was deluged with requests from nations of Asia, Africa, and Latin America which had not been included under the original criteria. To invite these countries would have meant expanding conference membership beyond all hope of tangible, concrete achievement. So it was decided that, although they could not all participate, the results of the conference would be made freely available to all the developing nations of the world.

The meeting was now to be the largest high-level conference, outside the United Nations, ever devoted to any aspect of economic development. It was to be the first such conference at which delegates from industrialized countries and underdeveloped nations would meet, discuss common problems, and explore ways in which they might help each other. And, as realization of the historic nature of this meeting grew, the level of representation rose. Almost every country sent a delegate of at least cabinet rank. There were three vice-presidents, several ministers of foreign affairs and finance, the Chef de Cabinet of the United Nations, and the Director of the ILO. The United States Delegation alone was headed by Vice-President Johnson and included the Secretary of Labor, the Secretary of HEW, the Chairman of the President's Council of Economic Advisers, the Chief of the State Department's Policy Planning Staff, and the Director of the Peace Corps.

But, despite the level and importance of this conference, and the beauty of its Puerto Rican surroundings, it was considered essential that this be a working meeting conducted on a scale consistent with Peace Corps traditions of dedicated austerity. Hotel rates were set at an average of $17 a day per delegate for room and three meals—less than it would have cost at a good hotel in the American Midwest or in Washington. No liquor or

cigarettes or the other frills so often associated with large conferences were provided out of taxpayers' money. A Puerto Rican
hotel was chosen which would permit all the delegates to live,
eat, and work in a small, completely self-contained area, so as
to eliminate the waste of time and confusion normally encountered in moving from hotel to restaurants to convention halls.
And, despite the fact that more than 160 representatives attended, the cost was far less than that of most conferences of
equivalent size.

The conference itself was exceptionally hard work. The average day began at nine in the morning and formal sessions
ended at eleven at night, with many delegates staying up until
one and two in the morning discussing and debating the issues
which had been raised. Although there were some complaints,
most of the participants agreed that the arduous sessions created
an atmosphere of intimate collaboration, a sense of urgency,
and a feeling of personal participation in the great questions
which were presented, which helped substantially to make the
conference a success.

But the final importance of this conference cannot be measured by low costs or long hours. What is important is the concrete, tangible result of the three days of discussion and the
many months of preparation.

In his statement announcing the Puerto Rican meeting,
President Kennedy expressed the hope that this conference
would prove a "milestone in the formulation of a strategy of
economic development." And, although the final results will
not be completely known for many years, I believe we have
already justified this hope.

In the eighteen years since the close of World War II, the
United States has been engaged, together with many other nations, in a vast and costly effort to assist developing nations in
an attack on the poverty, hunger, and ignorance which are their
ancient heritage. More money has been spent by nations to

help the development of others in these eighteen years than in all the centuries of previous recorded history. From this experience we have all learned much about the problems of development. Above all, we have learned that money alone does not bring progress; that without educated and trained men and women to man the factories, run the businesses, and guide the governments of developing nations, large capital investment only serves to arouse hopes which cannot be fulfilled. We cannot, as an American economist has written, build economic monuments in a sea of illiteracy and hope to bring permanent improvements in human welfare. Human progress is largely the result of human effort and human skill. And it became apparent to all who attended the Puerto Rican Conference that, unless we vastly increased our emphasis on the development of skilled manpower, the hopes of hundreds of millions for a better way of life were doomed to frustration—a frustration that would ultimately bring discontent and chaos and even greater misery.

If the conference had done nothing more than heighten this awareness and a determination to solve this problem, it would have been a success. But it accomplished far more than this. For it went on to develop specific measures and programs designed to make an immediate and significant contribution to the almost insatiable need for skilled manpower.

First, it called upon private enterprise, business, and labor to make available its huge storehouse of training, knowledge, and resources to the underdeveloped world. We were convinced that private enterprise would be willing, even eager, to offer its hard-won knowledge of techniques for the development of human skills. And, in response to this call, the Business Council for International Understanding, backed by the voluntary contributions of American industry, is already engaged in establishing three pilot training programs in widely diverse areas of the developing world.

Second, we assembled for the conference a large array of

newly developed techniques of training. For, in the field of human skills, as in so many other fields, modern science has been steadily developing new technologies and methods. Some of these technologies make it possible, for example, to transform an unskilled worker into a carpenter or mason or x-ray technician in a short period of time, bypassing many of the traditional methods of vocational and technical education. For the first time, these new technologies were assembled, presented, discussed, and made available to interested countries in the form of carefully designed and completely packaged model training centers. The conference gave to the International Labor Organization the responsibility of further disseminating information about these new techniques. And already several countries are in the process of negotiating for the establishment of training centers as part of their own programs of skill development.

Third, and perhaps most important, the conference gave an enormous impulse to the world-wide spread of the concept of volunteer service—the Peace Corps idea. For the success of the United States Peace Corps, and the work of the volunteer organizations of other countries, has demonstrated beyond doubt that dedicated men and women, moved by the desire to help others, carefully selected and trained to do needed work, can make an enormous contribution to the need for skilled manpower in economic development while, at the same time, increasing understanding and friendship among nations. The documents of this book bear almost unanimous witness to this fact.

Convinced of the value and urgency of the Peace Corps idea, the conference unanimously voted to establish a new international secretariat, charged with the responsibility of stimulating, encouraging, and coordinating an increased flow of volunteer assistance to the developing nations of the world. Largely as a result of the conference and the work of the secretariat, in the last few months four European nations and New Zealand have announced the formation of new volunteer organizations. Others are now studying such programs. Several other countries, convinced of the importance of their own volunteer work, have begun to expand earlier programs.

And, in the developing countries themselves, we have witnessed an increased awareness that the volunteer efforts of their own young men and women may well represent a hitherto untapped and enormously significant resource in the struggle for human dignity and a decent way of life. The Republic of Honduras has already announced its intention to form its own Peace Corps to work within its own borders. In Bolivia, in Chile, in Jamaica, and elsewhere, new organizations are coming to life—organizations designed to tap the enormous creative energy of men and women willing to dedicate their time, their energies, and their skills to the progress of their nations and the welfare of their fellow citizens.

And this is just the beginning. For the Peace Corps idea—the concept of volunteer service—has such enormous vitality and importance, such a radiating appeal to the imaginations and hopes of man, that I am convinced that it will eventually spread over many lands. From the Puerto Rican Conference will flow an ever-swelling torrent of men and women demonstrating with their own labors and determination that the future progress of nations lies with individuals freely giving of themselves to the welfare of their fellow men. By thus reaffirming the willingness of individuals to accept the often burdensome responsibilities of freedom and independence, they will reaffirm our faith in the capacity of individual man to shape the future of his family, his community, and his nation.

Why build these cities glorious
    If man unbuilded goes?
In vain we build the world, unless
    The builder also grows.
        —EDWIN MARKHAM

# Chapter

# I

# The 1962 San Juan Conference

A concept broad enough to affect global thinking has to grow out of experience. One day we recognize it and call it an idea; but until that time its maturing is a gradual process at best. Doubtless there is some moment—and we may or may not be aware of it—when the slowly mounting evidence for a hitherto overlooked principle reaches the "critical mass" necessary to gain our full conscious attention. Then, as often as not, it all seems so apparent that we wonder how we missed it before.

So it must have been with the concept of investment in human resources as a controlling factor in economic and social development. However basic, however obvious this principle may be now, it is useless for us to say that we knew it all the time; for, lip service aside, there is not too much to prove that we did and a good deal to suggest that we didn't. In our generation this concept, while we can see now that it germinated everywhere in plain view for at least two decades, can be said to have come to full maturity only within the last two years. Interestingly enough, in retrospect we can trace fairly well its course of development and the final convincing event that led to the first International Conference on Middle Level Manpower held in San Juan, Puerto Rico, in October of 1962.

## What Is Middle Level Manpower?

The term *middle level manpower* had not been in common use among manpower specialists before 1962, but it has now fixed itself in their literature. It has no very precise definition and, like people, no precise limits. It has no reference whatsoever to mediocre ability and is not to be confused with it, since it is an occupational rather than qualitative term. It refers generally to that wide category of vocationally skilled workers from which we exclude top management and the most highly trained professional people on the one hand, and unskilled labor on the other.

Individuals in the middle level occupations may have varying degrees of training and in many cases may be very highly skilled indeed in their specialties. Middle level manpower includes such people as teachers, nurses, factory and construction foremen, carpenters, electricians, machinists, masons, plumbers, laboratory technicians, engine and boiler operators, auto mechanics, heavy duty equipment operators, typists and secretarial workers. Men and women who have appropriate middle level skills are capable of understanding the operation and maintenance of machines, reading blueprints, scheduling work, following established procedures, working to standards of quality and performance.

Shortage of middle level manpower affects economic development in two ways. At the outset it retards actual physical construction—the building of dams, plants, schools—and even the efficient handling of sheer paper work connected with development programs. Then, when any of these factories, hospitals, power plants or transport systems are in fact completed, shortage of such manpower retards their operation, lowers their output, and increases their maintenance and operating cost. You may end up with schools, but with no teachers in them; hospitals, but no nurses to staff them; factories without skilled labor. The new projects may therefore prove uneconomical—or even, in some cases, inoperable.

These are the problems that for years have been faced and fought to varying extent by the developing nations and those assisting them. If the battle has not been won, at least a considerable body of knowledge has been built up in the collective experience of the various countries and assisting agencies. What has been the origin of this accumulating experience?

## The Background

Historically, the human resources problem that brought together this conference of nations actually began to take shape at the end of World War II. The war itself had much to do with it. Unprecedented advances in world communication and travel, mass movement and interchange of foreign troops, and similar corollary effects of a world-wide conflict brought to all countries an accelerated exposure to different cultures, and invited comparisons of the material well-being of other areas.

In those years the peoples of Asia, Africa, and Latin America began to awaken from ancient, changeless modes of life, from centuries of either political and economic domination from abroad or its domestic feudal equivalent, from ignorance and fear at home and from a deep-rooted distrust of the foreigner. Encouraged by the United Nations Charter's commitment to self-determination and self-government, the emerging nations began to look to a day of economic as well as political independence. And in this the developed nations, as co-authors of the Charter themselves and no less impressed with the existing imbalances, undertook to assist them as their abilities and resources would permit.

Experts journeyed everywhere, development surveys prolif-
erated, and soon ambitious national five-year plans dotted the
globe. Individually these plans reflected the hopes of each country, but all had one feature in common. The extraordinary
success of the Marshall Plan in rebuilding and restarting the
machinery of European progress led many to believe that similarly oriented programs would spark the economic growth
needed in the newly developing countries.

Thus it was taken as axiomatic that the primary, overshadow-
ing development requirement of these countries was financial
investment capital. The five-year plans were drawn up almost
exclusively in money terms, unavoidably perhaps, but at this
time mainly as allocations for physical capital works. For these
the United States, and soon other developed countries as well,
launched substantial programs of government financial aid, at
the same time encouraging their private citizens to consider
productive investments abroad. In the family of United Nations
affiliates the International Bank for Reconstruction and Development turned from its earlier assistance in the reconstruction
of war-torn Europe to the financing of self-liquidating physical
capital projects in its less-developed member countries.

To be sure, in all of this the importance of human know-how
was not forgotten. Technical experts to advise, organize, build
or launch various projects were made available in appreciable
numbers by the developed nations, both directly and through
the United Nations and its specialized agencies. Private investors brought their supervisors and production specialists with
them. Labor was available locally, and cheap.

Or was it? Wages were indeed low, producers found, but so
was output with unskilled workers. Projects did not move ahead
as fast as expected. The five-year plans, even when adequately
financed, failed to meet their targets. Engineers, money, and
tools could not build roads in the Middle East without construction foremen. Costly hydroelectric schemes could produce

power for lathes—which would not turn without operators. A tractor could do wonders on an Asian farm—until for want of skilled maintenance it broke down, and then all the cash in the world could not repair it without a mechanic. Money, the rich and the poor nations both learned, cannot buy electricians in the Andes or teachers in Central Africa. It can build hospitals and buy medical supplies, but it can't buy jungle nurses.

Gradually it began to be suspected that financial aid, no matter how massive, was not the ultimate answer to the development problems of the emerging nations. From the early 1950's onward there began to be a shift in emphasis, among professional economic development specialists, from the importance of physical capital investment and high-level technical assistance to the even greater role played by human skills and technology at the broad middle level. Nowhere was this more pronounced, perhaps, than in the authoritative economic development studies of major institutions of financial capital assistance—among them, in particular, the International Bank for Reconstruction and Development.[1]

In a World Bank report on the economic prospects of one member country, for example, the following observation was made:

The need for trained manpower, particularly technically trained people at the intermediate level with a secondary education or its equivalent, cannot be emphasized too strongly. Although there is not yet a systematic study of . . . manpower requirements, every person interviewed stated that this was the most critical manpower shortage. No matter what the field of activity—agriculture, industry, education, commerce, health, and all other services—the shortage of intermediate personnel will be felt increasingly unless vigorous measures are taken now. Unlike the primary graduate, whose ab-

---

[1] International Bank for Reconstruction and Development, *Middle Manpower in Developing Countries,* Technical Paper No. 13, International Conference on Middle Level Manpower; Peace Corps, Washington, D.C. (1962).

sorption into the economy at a wage commensurate with his expectations is doubtful, the secondary graduate will be in constant demand. In fact, it is difficult to imagine how the various sectors of the General Plan can meet their targets unless the supply of intermediate manpower is increased.

The same kind of report on another emerging country stated:

The maintenance of the rate of growth at five to six per cent a year in the economy as a whole, and the rate of ten per cent a year for the industrial sector particularly, will not be possible unless there is a considerable increase in the number of skilled workers, engineers, teachers, industrial managers and the like to meet the requirements of an expanding economy.

To quote just one more of many similar illustrations, not long ago the World Bank advised another of its member countries in reference to its national program that "educational expansion, particularly at the secondary level, must be regarded as the key to economic development."

*Early Efforts*

From the onset of these many development programs education was by no means overlooked. In almost all cases some financial provision was made for a stepped-up school program. Unfortunately at first this was generally no more than an expansion of the prewar local system, most frequently designed to turn out white-collar clerical assistants for a colonial administration or to prepare students for study abroad in certain socially popular professions—notably law. Moreover, the development funds for education itself tended to go largely into physical capital investment in the form of schoolhouses, often with less than adequate emphasis on the preparation of teachers for them.

At the same time quite a number of the developing countries chose to allocate sizable portions of their educational development funds to the creation or expansion of national universities. The long-term value of local universities as an ultimate solution to certain shortages in the higher ranks is undeniable, and some appreciable assistance in early staffing of such institutions through overseas aid and exchange programs proved feasible. But neither these nor the other efforts mentioned were directed at the most crucial manpower problem impeding the successive five-year plans. Summarizing more than a decade of intensive economic development studies throughout the less-developed areas, the World Bank only recently declared:

It is probably fair to say that in most cases the Bank has found that there is a tendency in its member countries to overspend on primary education, on the one hand, and university level institutions on the other, and to neglect the middle part of the structure, whether it be secondary education in the usual sense of the term or vocational or technical training.

The full meaning of such an observation made in 1962 is revealed only when one considers, first, the numerous earlier studies and reports such as the examples already quoted here; secondly, the practical difficulties experienced in meeting the targets of the various national economic development plans almost from their inception; and finally, the fact that many of these programs have been under way for ten or fifteen years, and some even longer. What is made clear is that throughout this period there was a growing awareness of the shortage of middle level skills but—as evident from the limited corrective measures —still not enough awareness to rate it as a problem of the first magnitude.

The final event that brought this into focus came from an unexpected quarter: the United States Peace Corps. True, the Peace Corps was not established to conduct economic development surveys, nor did it venture in any way to do so. But within its first year it had thousands of volunteers living and working directly with the people of twoscore developing nations, under conditions more intimate than had been possible in previous overseas aid programs. The first-hand observations of these many alert volunteers, coupled with the Peace Corps' unique system of constant professional field evaluation of its own work, brought home as never before the overriding urgency of middle level skill development in all these countries. And if this were not enough, the story was told once more in their pyramiding requests for more Peace Corps help, and yet again more forcefully in the predominant vocations and fields of work for which the volunteers were wanted. For of course it is inherent in the nature of the Peace Corps volunteer system, unlike earlier technical assistance programs, that it deals most closely with this broad area of middle level skills. It would be difficult indeed to miss the fundamental implication of these mounting demands.

Thus in the spring of 1962, when on behalf of the United States President John F. Kennedy issued invitations to nations of the free world to participate in a searching conference on this problem, he was in effect asking them to come together and answer the question: "Is it true, as we are beginning to suspect, that our joint economic development efforts have been concentrating too heavily in the wrong place—that we have been placing too much reliance on investment in things when perhaps we should be investing more in people?"

To the developing nations the answer to this question could determine how soon they could actually realize the goals of a better life for their millions of citizens. To the more developed countries, and particularly to the United States with its long-sustained assistance effort, it was certainly of no less concern. For one thing, a continued rapid expansion of the U.S. Peace Corps was clearly indicated and would be pursued in any event as fast as circumstances and resources permitted; but obviously the mere size of the job to be done simultaneously in so many newly emerging countries threatened eventually to tax this one localized source of initial middle manpower aid beyond its capacity. The problem, whatever its answer, was one requiring the concerted knowledge, experience and effort of the entire community of nations.

### Organization of the San Juan Conference

Appropriately Puerto Rico, as a developing country with an outstanding record of achievement in this field, was chosen as the scene of the 1962 conference on "Human Skills in the Decade of Development." In the busy months beforehand preparations were handled in Washington by an interagency committee headed by Conference Secretary-General William F. Haddad, Associate Director of the Peace Corps, and Richard N. Goodwin, U.S. Deputy Assistant Secretary of State for Inter-American Affairs, aided by a fully staffed professional secretariat supplied by the United States.

As part of the preparations the secretariat solicited informative technical papers from participating governments, major international bodies, and prominent authorities in the manpower field. A number of special studies were conducted and reported. Extensive bibliographies of the subject were prepared with the assistance of the U.S. Library of Congress and other agencies. For the assistance of the conference delegates these documents, research papers and studies of manpower development programs from various parts of the world were published and made available in English, Spanish, and French,[2] the official languages in which the conference discussions were conducted simultaneously. In addition, through the assistance of the Office of Technical Services of the U.S. Department of Commerce, a very extensive library on manpower problems and modern training

---

[2] For bibliographies and a list of these conference papers see Appendices 2 and 3.

methods was assembled at the actual conference site for use by the delegates.

From the preliminary studies it was agreed that the San Juan Conference should have the following over-all objectives:

1. To discuss and evaluate world-wide shortages of middle level manpower as an important obstacle to rapid social and economic development;

2. To make possible international consideration of the shortage of middle level manpower and techniques of assessing this shortage in each nation;

3. To examine methods for rapidly increasing and improving the training of middle level manpower within the developing countries, including the examination of new technologies of training and the establishment of training programs outside the framework of formal education;

4. To discuss methods whereby the industrialized countries can initiate and expand programs to supply volunteer assistance to ease the shortages in other nations;

5. To discuss techniques whereby volunteer assistance can be used to help convert unskilled labor surplus into trained middle level manpower; and the use of volunteers of the developing country in the development of their own nation;

6. To discuss methods of continuing international cooperation in order to bring all available resources to bear most effectively upon the training and supply of middle level manpower.

### Tone of the Discussions

Following the opening of the conference by Peace Corps Director Sargent Shriver and a welcome on behalf of Puerto Rico extended by Governor Luis Muñoz Marín to the forty-three nations, nine international organizations, and seven private agencies represented,[3] the Conference delegates elected as their

---

3 For the list of nations, organizations, delegates, and observers see Appendix 1.

chairman U.S. Vice-President Lyndon B. Johnson, with Vice-President Emmanuel Pelaez of the Philippines as Co-Chairman. In his keynote address to the opening session Vice-President Johnson suggested guidelines for discussion when he said:

"We [in the U.S.] have found three factors upon which we believe we can build for future action. The first is the willingness of skilled individuals in many countries to spend part of their lives imparting their skills to others. The second is the recent development of rapid training techniques which can help in filling the middle manpower gap within the shortest possible time. The third is the reservoir of experience built up by private industry in its never-ending search for skilled workers to meet the demands of ever-changing technology."

If the conference could find the means for concerted action to take advantage of these three assets, the Vice-President said, it would make a major contribution to this Decade of Development; and he drew upon American history to clarify a point of frequent misunderstanding.

"America's prosperity," he said, "has often been mistakenly attributed solely to our possession of great stores of natural resources. It is true that we are blessed in that respect, but it is not the whole story. Part of the credit can be traced to the fact that we started only recently—in historical terms—to develop virgin territory; and part must go to certain prudent laws passed a number of years ago." He mentioned as specific examples the Morrill Land Act of 1862 creating support for colleges of agriculture and mechanical arts, and the Smith-Lever Act of 1914 establishing the national system of agricultural extension agents.

"If we turn to Asia," he continued, "the striking fact is that the most prosperous countries—Israel and Japan—are relatively poor in natural resources. They have flourished by developing their human resources."

Touching on the work of the Peace Corps, Vice-President

Johnson spoke of the realization that one's own prosperity is bound together with the prosperity of others. "Therefore," he said, "we feel the need to share with others whatever skills modern science and technology have brought to us, and we hope that others will share their skills with us. We are long since past the historic point where nations can live in isolation. . . . We seek to pool our experiences, to the end that our activity is not only inspired by humanitarianism but is purposefully directed and effective."

The ensuing discussions explored from a multitude of aspects the six general conference objectives already listed, and in particular the three factors stressed by the chairman. As will be evident in later pages, many informative experiences and useful concrete suggestions were made available by the individual participating countries. Beyond these, however, three larger themes suffused the discussions from beginning to end.

First among them is that the development of a country requires the emergence of an authentic sense of individual engagement in the national effort. As Vice-President Johnson has expressed it, "The key to success within the developing nation lies not merely in the realm of technical activity. It lies in bringing the city folk and the country folk, the rich and the poor, the scholar and the illiterate, all into a sense of common purpose and common nationhood."

Second is the growing consciousness in developing areas that the problem of development is a common task for all nations, and that in fulfillment of this task there are values and responsibilities of equal importance for the nations which give and the nations which receive development assistance. One striking disclosure of the discussions is an awareness that, out of diverse experiences, the developing nations are increasingly capable of assisting one another.

Finally, it is becoming ever clearer that no aspect of the joint development effort is more likely to build this sense of common purpose than the face-to-face requirements of the process of creating and diffusing human skills. We are very quickly learning that the freely arranged interchange of men and women in these development tasks is making an unprecedented contribution, not only to the tasks themselves but to international brotherhood and understanding.

It is not improbable, therefore, that the 1962 conference at San Juan will mark a turning point in the course of international development assistance, toward greater emphasis on human development and less on the supposed magic of mere money and hardware.

### The Ensuing Chapters

What follows in the balance of this volume, toward showing the basis for this conclusion, is not in any sense a transcript of the conference. Rather, it is a form of report which seeks to draw together from the various parts of the conference record a fair picture of the present overall thinking, by the many participating national and international leaders and professional authorities, on the crucial questions for which the conference was called. It is accordingly presented, not as a chronological narrative account, but as a digest of today's views on these questions as disclosed by the San Juan discussions.

# Chapter

# II

# How Important Are Human Beings to Economic Development?

Today's universal interest in speeding the growth of the less developed economies has thrown into bold relief the high rates of return realized on investments in training and education. Of what avail are engines without engineers? Or machinery without machinists?

Technology can be imported, but technicians and scientists must be trained. Nor can one simply start at the top of the pyramid. Its base must be built by an educational system that reduces illiteracy and diffuses knowledge.

Why has human capital now moved out of the chorus and to the front of the stage? How much shall we invest in machines, and how much in people? Walter Heller, Chairman of President Kennedy's Council of Economic Advisers, has some answers to these questions. In the main, this is what Dr. Heller has to say:

# MEN, MONEY, AND MATERIALS

WALTER HELLER

*Chairman, U.S. Council of Economic Advisers*

In 1862 J. T. Rogers (in *The Journal of the Royal Statistical Society*) might have been writing for us a hundred years later when he argued that it is "unphilosophical to ignore capital in the person of a laborer and to recognize it in a machine" and that "The economist, for the advancement of his science, may well treat the human being simply as an investment of capital, in productive force." So the thoughts that guide our efforts in this field are not new. What *is* new is the weaving of the human capital factor into the fabric of economic development—into its theory and practice. We have arrived at a stage of some understanding and quantitative analysis of the role of human resources in economic development. Certainly we still have much to learn; but it is not too early to begin to translate our findings into practical policy terms.

Why do we now emphasize education's role in economic as well as social development?

One answer is that nations have become increasingly concerned with problems of growth and the process that underlies it. To analyze and understand the secrets of more rapid growth, we must search and understand the record of the past. We must know not only where we are, but how we got here. For we have learned that the rate of economic growth is not fixed by the laws of nature; rather, it is a variable which can within limits be bent to the will, the laws, and the policies of man. The evidence steadily mounts that the economic and social policies which govern the supply, the skills, and the attitudes of productive manpower lie at the base of the growth process.

### The Return on Investment in Human Beings

Recent studies by eminent authorities in different countries have yielded some revealing—and remarkably similar—data and conclusions on the role of human resources in economic development.

Among economists the most widely used method of measuring the contribution of human capital to economic growth is the so-called *"residual" approach*. For a given period of time one measures (1) the increases in total national output compared with (2) the increases in inputs of land, labor (man-hours worked), and physical capital. While the problems of measurement are by no means trivial, the basic idea is simple and the result is illuminating. In country after country the growth in output exceeds, by a wide margin, the growth in measured inputs of land, labor, and tangible capital. This "unexplained" part of growth is called the "residual"—that part of the rise in gross national product that is generated by such intangible factors as education, training, and research.

A series of studies for the United States shows that about half of the increase in output over the last fifty years must be attributed to factors other than the increase in the stock of tangible capital and man-hours worked. These are startling results, for it seems only a few years ago that most laymen and many economists believed the "secret" of U.S. growth to lie almost entirely in its great investment in physical capital and its rich endowment of natural resources. To be sure, it is only through physical investment that technology and brain power can be translated into production and growth. But the recent pioneering research indicates that, insofar as the separate productive factors can be isolated, capital investment *per se* accounts for only between 10 and 20 percent of the increased output per unit of labor input.

Nor is the United States unique in this regard. Other economies, too, have grown far more rapidly than can be explained by the increases in measured input. In Latin America, for example, average economic growth for the period 1945-1955 is estimated at 4.9 percent per year, but the measured increase in inputs averaged only 3.1 percent; so an impressive residual of 1.8 percent traces to education and other "intangible inputs." Studies for a longer period in Norway (1900-1955) arrived at the identical figure of 1.8 percent annual increase in output unaccounted for by the increeces in labor and capital. For Finland, the corresponding figure for the years 1925-1952 was found to be 1.2 percent.

An even more dramatic story unfolds when the analysis is limited to the agricultural sector. Here the U.S. experience from 1940 to 1958 is startling: with an increased input of only 1.7 percent *per decade,* output increased by 29 percent. For several Latin American countries also we have impressive results: Argentina (1920-1940), inputs per decade up 6 percent, output up 27.5 percent; Brazil (1925-29 to 1945-49), inputs up 15 percent, output up 27 percent; Mexico (1925-29 to 1945-49), inputs up 13.5 percent, output up 30 percent.

Beyond telling us that capital isn't everything, these figures mean that we finally have some measure of the contribution to economic development of the intangible inputs: upgrading of the skills and knowledge of the labor force, improvements in organization and management, advances in technology, and economies of scale. Most of these inputs originate in education and training.

The findings, even taken cautiously, range from the impressive to the spectacular. In the United States, growing investment in formal education is estimated to account for one-fourth to one-half of the "residual"—the 1.6 percent annual growth in output that cannot be attributed to inputs of tangible capital and labor. Of course more research is needed, particularly in developing economies, before we can calculate rates of return on investment in human skills and knowledge as confidently as we calculate the pay-off on investments in machines, equipment, and plant. But the basic lesson—that investments in human capital offer high returns—is inescapable. It must be built into our development programs and growth policies as a central ingredient.

### Direct Returns from Education

The lesson is driven home even more pointedly by measurements of the direct increases in individual incomes associated with increases in education. In this way, too, it is possble to calculate a rate of return on investment in education. Income is one measure of the individual's contribution to a nation's production. The effect of education on the national output can therefore be assessed, at least in part, by measuring the relationship between education and income—and, by inference, productivity.

The rate of return on investment in college education in the United States has been found to be roughly comparable to the rate of return on business investment. Similar studies show that the rate of return on elementary and high school education combined is substantially greater than that for higher education. Furthermore, in the newly developing countries where educated manpower is more scarce, evidence indicates that the marginal contribution of a well-educated and trained individual to the economy is even greater. A Venezuelan study, for example, yields rates of return on investment in education which are sharply above those for the United States. Actually all of these studies understate the real rate of return since they make no allowance for that part of educational cost which represents consumption. Nor do they allow for that important additional part of educational return which we class as indirect, or third-party, or neighborhood benefits.

A practical consequence of this growing body of research is that, in the future, ministries of education and of labor will be equipped with more and more rigorous evidence as to the pay-off on investment in their areas. They will be able to argue in much the same documented, convincing terms as ministers of agriculture, transportation and power have in the past. This is as it should be, although we may extend our sympathies to the finance ministers defending their treasuries against such an irresistible onslaught.

## The Development of Policy Guides

The figures just cited are the results of careful, detailed scientific research on the importance of human resources. Many countries can corroborate these findings out of their own experiences. Many, too, know of plans and projects that had to be "put on the shelf" not because capital was lacking, not because labor was in short supply—but simply because the *skills* needed to carry out the plans, to operate the machines, were unavailable.

It is not enough, however, to agree that a lack of training and education can set limits upon the growth rate of the economy and even upon the importation of physical capital. It is not enough merely to be in favor of more education, more training, more skilled manpower. We need to know how to achieve these goals. We need operating principles to guide our policy decisions. And to arrive at them we must consider continuously and realistically such factors as national capabilities for developing manpower, new techniques of training and retraining, the role of volunteer services in meeting immediate shortages, the role of the private sector in training, and the role of the developed nations in general.

In the language of the economist, we have to face hard problems of choice in determining both our *total* investment in human capital and the optimum *composition* of our education and training efforts. What pattern of knowledge and skills is best suited to our economic and social aspirations? And how best can we supply or produce that pattern? There are no easy, universal answers, since decisions must be based on varying circumstances. But cutting across time and space are certain issues that the policy makers of *every* country must meet. Only as we face them squarely and resolve them wisely will we develop reliable policy guides for investing in education and training.

1. First, at the most general level: *What is the profitable rate and emphasis of investments in human capital relative to investments in physical capital?* The evidence cited strongly supports some shift in emphasis from physical to human capital in development programming. This shift requires the most careful forethought because the "payoff period" on general education— and even on training for skills—is longer, and the benefits less tangible, than when we invest in machines and brick-and-mortar. And identifying the shortages and surpluses of manpower—not just today's but tomorrow's—is more difficult. Yet, unless the rate of increase in human capital is well above the rate of growth; unless the strategic middle and upper level manpower is growing two or three times as fast as the labor force; unless education and training are overcoming shortages of technicians, craftsmen, teachers, nurses, and the like while reducing surpluses of unskilled and obsolescent labor—unless these tests are met, the ministries of education, labor, and development are falling short of their job.

2. Second, *what is the best allocation of resources among primary, secondary, vocational, and higher education?* In the present discussion we are concerned mainly with middle level manpower as the undernourished segment of our skill structure. When willing hands are idle because they lack needed skills, the nation loses. And it also loses when the economist works as a statistical clerk, when the engineer becomes a mechanic, when the physician must also act as nurse and laboratory technician.

We know that many nations have a gap between the unskilled and top-level manpower. Filling it should be a basic part of their programs for economic growth.

3. *What incentives can help to correct imbalances in our skill structure?* We may identify shortages, and develop and finance training programs to meet them, but the rewards in terms of personal satisfaction, status, or pay must be high enough to attract people into these programs. A wage structure tightly bound by custom and tradition often invites imbalance in the labor force. Opening it to market forces—enabling it to respond to the forces of supply and demand and productivity—will help pull manpower into the channels where the economy most needs it. Government itself can sometimes play a direct role, by realigning its own pay scales to reflect as accurately as possible a realistic assessment of manpower priorities in a developing economy.

4. *What role should the private sector play?* Broadly, we view "education" as the process of imparting general knowledge and developing basic mental ability, and "training" as the teaching of more specific skills for particular kinds of jobs. In this sense, education with its large external or social benefits must be very largely a government responsibility. But training, which offers a direct and often large return to both employee and employer, can in substantial part be provided privately—not necessarily without government guidance and assistance, but primarily at private expense.[1]

5. *How can outside manpower be used as a source of scarce skills?* To fill manpower gaps by importing skilled manpower from abroad is characteristic of the earlier phases of development programs. But, Peace Corps aside, it is an expensive way of doing the job. It should be viewed not as a substitute for, but as an instrument for, development of a skilled local labor

[1] This and other aspects of the private sector's role are discussed from the viewpoints of various participating nations in Chapter V.

supply. The greatest profit will be realized from imported manpower if it is used principally to convey skills and knowledge to its domestic counterparts—creating, as it were, a "human counterpart fund" to leave as a living legacy.

These are not the only issues, of course. Each national development program faces others no less important, either common to all or perhaps dictated by local conditions. For instance, how should education and training efforts be divided between the rural and urban sectors? How can enough flexibility be maintained in manpower preparation, in an era of rapid economic and technological advance, to strike a proper balance between anticipation of future needs and quick response to unexpected developments? How can new accelerated training techniques best be used to accomplish more in less time? These and similar questions must be answered by every developing country in selecting the best investment portfolio in human capital.

## THE MANPOWER FACTOR

### REVIEW OF CONFERENCE DISCUSSIONS

As we have just seen from Dr. Heller's remarks, the findings of recent years demonstrate that in our preoccupation with physical capital works we have until today tended to underestimate grossly the contribution of human capital to economic growth. The preceding discussion has emphasized, however, that we have some distance to go before we can hope to measure this factor with precision. The present stage of economic research gives us only an approximate, though useful, index of its relative importance in economic development planning.

For those who would pursue these computations further, a scholarly critique of the various methods appears in a confer-

24 : THE HIDDEN FORCE

ence document [2] by Professor Irvin Sobel of Washington University. Pointing out the interplay of numerous indeterminate side effects, and some of the supplementary influences that methods to date still fail to take into account adequately, Professor Sobel reaffirms with supporting detail Dr. Heller's warning that much more research remains to be done before mathematical conclusions in this field can be taken as accurate indices. But, he says, "Despite its obvious defects the so-called residual approach confirms what many of us in the economic development field in general and in the manpower field in particular have long believed: that increase in accumulation of physical capital has played neither a unitary nor even a dominant role in economic development." Furthermore, he adds, "The results obtained through the various measures, even though average rather than marginal rates of return, consistently display a higher rate of return at all levels for investment in human resources as opposed to other investment alternatives."

*Pakistan's Firsthand Experience*

Some very interesting empirical support of this conclusion is offered by Joint Secretary Zahiruddin Ahmed of Pakistan's Finance Ministry. He compares his country's own practical experiences with two consecutive five-year development plans, the first of which ran from 1955 to 1959. Making due allowances for the fact that the budget of the first five-year plan was about half that of the current plan now being carried out, Pakistan has found that the rate of growth during the first period was very much smaller than should have been expected, judging by what has been achieved during the present program. Says Mr. Ahmed: "The difference is not because larger financial re-

---

[2] Sobel, Irvin, *Relationship Between Education and Productivity: An Analysis of Approaches and Studies,* Technical Paper No. 4, International Conference on Middle Level Manpower; Peace Corps, Washington, D.C. (1962).

sources are now available to us. Actually, relative to the sizes of the two plans, the position in regard to financial and material resources has not really undergone a very significant change; proportionately we have had more or less the same availability of such resources. What has really changed during this period is the human element—the element of manpower, the training that our people have received, the skills that they have developed and their ability to carry through the development program.

"Now, the result of this increase in the skills of our people has been a multiplied effect. The increase [in growth] has not been in direct proportion to the increase in the financial input of the development effort; it has been much larger. This, seemingly, goes directly to prove the thesis that the invisible inputs, those that get into the development effort as a result of increased human skills, produce much larger results than do the inputs of physical resources like finances and technical equipment."

Mr. Ahmed assures us that as a professional financier himself he is well aware of the traditional competitive battle between government ministries for development funds in any country. But, he declares, finance ministers are beginning to realize very much the importance of human skills in the development effort, and they know that money put into the training of human manpower will bring results. "They have come to realize during the passage of years that money abroad is not such a scarce resource. They are beginning to realize that money can be begged, borrowed if necessary, or sometimes even stolen. But that is not the case with human assets. It takes years and years of training before you can produce a skilled man. You cannot borrow, beg or steal human skills. And with this realization, the finance ministries of the various developing countries are beginning to lay more adequate emphasis on the development of manpower skills. . . . It is now becoming fairly universally recognized among the developing countries that human resources are as important, if not more important, than other resources for progress in the development effort."

Accordingly, Mr. Ahmed feels that the real question is not whether manpower development is crucial, but what to do about it. Once Pakistan started attacking the manpower question it soon encountered the common problem that "What is everybody's business is nobody's business"; in short, manpower planning tended to get neglected because there was no central agency with definite responsibility in this field. Pakistan's answer to this problem, as well as the solutions of other countries to similar difficulties, will be dealt with in the following chapter. Other related problems and experiences in such matters as the choice of training methods, and in the encouragement of assistance by the private sector, will be discussed in Chapters IV and V.

### Waste of Manpower

A point closer to the present discussion, raised incidentally by Mr. Ahmed in outlining the central objectives of national manpower planning, is the factor of wastage. In a different connection this factor is put forward also by Jamaica's Minister of Development and Welfare, Mr. Edward Seaga. Referring to lack of training as a major cause for unemployment, Mr. Seaga proposes that this type of human wastage should be measured, perhaps in terms of the difference between what a nation is producing and what it could produce if its unemployed were employed. He makes the challenging suggestion that the value of this factor should be introduced in computing the rate of return on national investment in education and training.

Pakistan's expressed concern with the wastage factor, however, deals with another aspect that is touched upon many times throughout these pages—that of forced underutilization of rare skills already possessed. "In places where a middle level man could do the job," says Mr. Ahmed, "often because of the lack of the proper middle level manpower we have had to employ a person of high level, of which we have a great shortage. As a result of nondevelopment in some of the middle level categories, there is a good deal of wastage that we have experienced in this way."

India regards the elimination of this kind of waste as one of the earliest points of attack in a national manpower program. An Indian Government paper[3] calls attention to the fact that increasing the supply of technical personnel, although of fundamental importance, is only a long-term solution. Among the faster measures that can be taken to cope with shortages of skilled manpower, it seems that the better use of the personnel already available is the most important.

## Middle Manpower in Management

Some developing countries currently view the scarcity of middle level skills primarily as an aspect of the management problem. One of these is the Ivory Coast, whose National Assembly President Philippe Yace declares, "The shortage of management personnel at the middle level is for us the major obstacle, because apart from our technical underdevelopment the Ivory Coast has most of the conditions that are necessary for rapid evolution." A similar thought is voiced by Tanganyika's Amir Habib Jamal, Minister of Communications, Power and Works, who even suggests that the presence of middle level management may be taken as an index of growth. "It is clear," he says, "that the very absence of skilled supervisory personnel in various fields is an indication of a lack of economic activity."

---

3 Government of India, *Elements of a Manpower Program for a Developing Country: The Indian Experience,* Technical Paper No. 5, International Conference on Middle Level Manpower; Peace Corps, Washington, D.C. (1962).

Citing as illustrations such countries as Japan, Holland, and Switzerland to show that a nation possessing a skilled work force can reach a very high level of economic advancement even if it does not have very great natural resources of its own, India puts the manpower factor first among the major ingredients of development. Indeed, says her government, "The main hope for the newly developing countries to attain a rapid rate of economic advancement, and to raise the living standards of their people in the foreseeable future, lies in the development of their human resources."

Just how much the manpower factor can affect not only the development rate, but even the direction of development, is shown by some figures from an Indian manpower survey. In planning for additional electric power on the basis of local experience to date, the Indian study finds that the operation of hydroelectric generating stations requires an average of 42 engineers of all levels for each 100,000 kw of installed capacity. Against this, for the same amount of installed power capacity, thermoelectric stations need 54 engineers and diesel installations demand 376. The phrasing of the study's conclusions suggests that, although the original installation costs are not identical, India will think twice before planning any new power development that does not provide the best use of scarce engineers.

With these and similar observations offered by many other countries, it is clear that few parts of the world any longer imagine physical investment capital to be the primary secret of development. Indeed, Dennis F. Vosper, United Kingdom Secretary for Technical Cooperation, goes so far as to suggest that perhaps the developed nations now supplying overseas assistance to other countries should devote somewhat less of their available resources to capital needs, and rather more to technical assistance and the general development of skilled manpower abroad. While acknowledging that this might be controversial, he suggests the possibility that in past years the latter aspect may have been comparatively neglected in relation to actual need. Britain, at any rate, currently devotes only 15 percent of its overseas aid expenditure to technical assistance. "I do not think that proportion is high enough, and I think it should be raised," Mr. Vosper declares, indicating that it was for this reason that only last year the government set up his department, which is concerned solely with technical assistance and not with capital aid.

Summarizing the broader aspects of human investment David Morse, Director General of ILO, stresses the implications of growth of the individual in society as a whole, and introduces some additional considerations in the general remarks that follow.

## THE HUMAN FACTOR IN PERSPECTIVE

DAVID A. MORSE

*Director General, International Labour Organization*

We have learned the lesson that although new financial investment is of course necessary in developing countries, it may be ineffective, or even wasteful, if there is not present the capacity to use capital. This capacity to use it includes, chief and foremost, the education and skills in the labor force of the kind needed to make new equipment productive. Thus the lack of competent trained personnel is, as so many have now come to recognize, a central problem in nearly every field of economic and social development and in nearly every developing country.

The magnitude of this problem may be gauged by the fact that the greatest percentage of the world's population is still illiterate, and a similar proportion of the world's children do not attend school. If between the developed and the newly developing areas of the globe the disparity in income levels is extreme, the contrasts in educational levels are no less so.

For instance, in the United States and the USSR together, there are more young men and women enrolled in institutions of higher education than in the rest of the world combined, and twice as many as in the whole of Africa, Asia, and Latin America put together. There are more than 3,500,000 students enrolled in technical schools in Japan and Western Germany, but only a little more than 500,000 in all of South America with a combined population almost as large. The low level of education and training in many countries today indicates not only how far they are from achieving modernization, but also how difficult it will be for them to develop rapidly. To eliminate this bottleneck, developing countries will have to accomplish in years what required centuries in the countries of Western Europe and North America.

As developing countries begin to examine their manpower needs more analytically and to make more reliable forecasts, we are beginning to get a clearer picture of the specific shortages. But if the gaps in middle level personnel are ultimately to be filled on a basis that is satisfactory to the countries concerned, the efforts already being exerted in most developing countries to assess manpower resources, to forecast manpower needs, and to institute appropriate training must be very greatly intensified. And in many areas there will have to be some corollary adjustments as well.

United Nations Secretary General U Thant, in his 1962 report on the UN Development Decade, summarized the position of the United Nations family on the development problem in declaring that, "In the years to come, national and international efforts must be concentrated on three major aspects of human resources development to which the highest priority must be attached: (1) better utilization of the labor force by creating higher levels of productive employment; (2) improving the quality of the labor force by vocational educational and training; (3) enlisting popular support for the tasks of national development, and the participation of broad social groups in them." His last point especially is worth some further comment, lest its full meaning escape.

It is common today, in many areas of the world, to find a real prejudice against manual work amongst those who have received an education. This attitude often applies even to graduates of vocational and technical schools; the educated man wants a white-collar job. It is particularly paradoxical in countries desperately short of skilled manpower, in that the longer a man remains at a technical school, the more highly trained he becomes, the less likely he is to be employed in the occupation for which he has been trained. From the very beginning of primary education, a determined effort must be made to inculcate positive attitudes toward manual work and to enhance the prestige and dignity of manual work throughout the economy, throughout the community.

It is also essential to envisage training within the wider context of a society changing in all its aspects. Of course this is true in any society, but it is particularly true in countries going through the transition from a traditional to an industrial way of life. What superficially may seem to be simple technological innovations are often in reality radical changes in ways of organizing human cooperation, of living and of thinking.

For instance, to transform a nomadic people, amongst whom cattle are regarded as a symbol of social prestige rather than an economic asset, into a settled community of dairy farmers cannot be done by purely "technical" training. It requires a complex series of changes in the customs and the attitudes and the institutions of these people which will probably require a considerable period of time to consolidate.

Since the chief task to be performed is really that of changing the attitudes of people, the help, assistance, and cooperation of young, objective, enthusiastic individuals may often be more useful than those of highly experienced specialists in achieving the objective of getting these people to accept new skills, new jobs, the notion of dignity of work, and new approaches to social and economic responsibility. And in the process—as such enterprises as the Peace Corps know well—those who have something to teach will find that they have something to learn.

The problem of education and training is fundamental to the problem of freedom in modern society. The essence of freedom is a sense of mastery over one's own destiny. Nothing so undermines this sense as the feeling of being lost in a strange, impersonal world, the creature of forces which can be neither understood nor controlled. This is the predicament in which workers coming from traditional communities may very well find themselves in taking up jobs in an industrial town: nothing in their traditional culture prepares them for the shock of a modern, impersonal industrial society. And it is in such despair that men are most likely to look to a self-appointed savior for an illusory deliverance.

So the fundamental task of education and training is to combat these enslaving tendencies, to give men the power of understanding which can make them free. And this brings us to the ultimate question of human resources in economic development: what is the place of man? Does man exist for economic development and higher production? Or is economic progress the means for greater happiness for men? The way we answer will determine the means we use to further economic growth, the kind of education and training we provide for individuals, and the type of society we are prepared to live in.

# Chapter

# III

## Manpower Planning—Why and How

All developing nations start with a work force composed predominantly of subsistence farmers with handicraft skills. The distance traveled by each country from this starting point measures the degree of development it has achieved. The distance it still has to travel before the larger portion of its work force consists of people equipped with middle level skills of today measures the magnitude of its further needs. The task, then, is to determine in each case how best and most speedily we may negotiate that distance.

One of the developing nations which has made substantial progress along this road is the Philippines. Its Vice-President Emmanuel Pelaez, Co-Chairman of the San Juan Conference, analyzes the process into its basic components in telling of his country's advance.

# ELEMENTS OF TRANSFORMATION

EMMANUEL PELAEZ

*Vice-President and Secretary of Foreign Affairs
of the Philippines*

As one of the developing countries, the Philippines has increasingly realized that growth demands something more than the construction of roads, the establishment of power facilities, or the building of steel mills and fertilizer plants. It demands the transformation of people. Underlying the statistical indicators of growth—the climbing gross national product, the rising rate of investment, the increase in employment and productivity—there must be a fundamental revolution of values, motivation, attitudes, work habits and skills. Most developing countries have embarked on programs of deliberate forced-pace development. These programs must include no less deliberate forced-pace transformation of the work force into a modern commercial-industrial labor pool.

For the change from the subsistence farm to the agricultural enterprise, from the village handicraft to the modern factory, from primitive trading to modern marketing, from moneylending to banking, from the communal to the corporate organization—all this is not just a matter of introducing modern equipment and large industrial plants. First and foremost, any such change involves the development of the manpower that will design and build the plants, operate and maintain the machinery, introduce modern agricultural techniques, and provide the manifold ancillary services that an industrial society requires.

In short, the work force must be changed from mere numbers to a catalogue of skills. There are three elements in this transformation:

*First,* as has already been commented, a fundamental change in values, motivations, and habits is needed. Traditional values and lackadaisical attitudes which are the combined products of a rural community and an older colonialism must be replaced by a new set of concepts and behavior patterns attuned to the demands of a dynamic society.

*Second,* manpower must have an opportunity to develop a new set of skills. A modern labor force requires certain basic educational disciplines. To be prepared for training in industrial skills, the worker must understand some of the basic concepts of modern physics, chemistry, biology, and be acquainted with the empirical methods of positive science.

*Third,* we must find productive outlets for these skills so they will improve the quality of life.

Unfortunately, this transformation all too often takes place in an unbalanced way. In most of the developing countries the aspiration for a fuller life has spread more rapidly than the development of the skills, the discipline, the personal motivation for more productive effort. Where the desire to break away from a rural community has produced an exodus to the urban centers, the facilities for transforming raw, unskilled, undisciplined manpower into a skilled labor force have not grown fast enough. And even where facilities for training have developed, a misallocation of content in relation to the substantive requirements of a balanced economic pattern has hampered the effort.

To remedy this weakness, we must do some basic planning. First, we need to make an estimate of the special skills that the future course of development in a country will demand; second, we have to examine and select the most efficient tools and facilities for developing those skills; and third, we must establish a framework of inducement and motivation that will draw people into the skills required. We cannot simply assume that this will all happen without consciously thinking it out. Forethought and integrated programs are required.

## The Demonstration Effect

Let us look at one example of what can happen if we do not calculate these steps carefully in advance. We have all been struck by the impact of the phenomenon which economists call the "demonstration effect" in the transformation of consumption patterns. This device has played a major role in the transformation of the Filipino people. But many of our problems have arisen precisely because the demonstration effect of superior consumption has been far more effective than the demonstration effect of superior production methods. Our farmer associates prosperity not with successful farming but with migration to the city.

Our experience then, dramatizes both the efficacy and the danger of demonstration as an agent of change—efficacy because the creation of desire for a new pattern has proven itself an effective solvent of traditional values and customary inertia; and danger, because the demonstration effect of this consumption pattern must be balanced by the demonstration of new and more efficient production methods. If we do not link the two in some kind of systematic program, the consumer aspirations of the population rise more rapidly than its capability to increase production and productivity.

In the Philippines, we have made headway over the past fifteen years. Our work force has undergone fairly significant changes. The basic aspirations of the new generation of rural people have turned radically toward city life. Business is no longer a disdained profession reserved only to aliens; indeed, the businessman has become the new "ilustrado" in our country today. Although too many of the young students flocking out of their villages into the urban centers still train for white-collar jobs, we now can see the beginnings of a movement toward the mechanical skills. The traditional prejudice against manual labor is giving way to new values that accord social prestige to technicians and tradesmen. This tendency has been stimulated by the rapid industrial development of the last twelve years, which saw the rise of enrollment in technical and business schools and the establishment of textile mills, automotive plants, appliance assembly factories, chemical establishments, flour mills, cement plants, and other industries.

Given the strategic position that the need for manpower development occupies in a program of economic growth, the task deserves the earnest attention of all nations which are concerned with narrowing the wide gap that now exists between wealthy and poor countries. This is an area where international collaboration can prove of tremendous value. Such collaboration is important not only in providing the developing nations with a forum for exchanging experiences in the technical methods of projecting manpower requirements, but particularly in expanding the scope and increasing the capability of action programs. For example, the task of retraining the pools of unemployed liberal arts and law school graduates in some of the developing countries can be made easier if they are exposed to a new environment wherein the opportunities open to new skills can be dramatized.

### Transformation at the National Level

As we consider the formulation of a new and enlarged program for international collaboration in the more rapid development of middle manpower skills, our focus should be on effective individual country programs. Starting from the elements of a sound country program, we can determine the extent to which regional and international programs can supplement the individual country's efforts to transform its working force.

At the individual country level, one can envision three key elements:

*First,* many of the developing countries either have or will probably establish manpower planning and development offices responsible for assessing the future manpower requirements of the economy and for working out development and training programs to supply the requirements.

*Second,* we will need to strengthen our formal educational systems to ensure a sound basic education for the population. It is clear that men and women entering the labor force must at least be able to read with comprehension, express themselves clearly and effectively, and use simple mathematical processes accurately.

*Third,* technical training, either formally through special vocational schools or more informally through training programs within industries, will have to be energized.

In each of these areas, collaboration among countries at various levels will prove extremely valuable. Permanent regional and international offices can provide a forum for the regular and systematic exchange of ideas and comparison of country experiences. For this specific purpose there should undoubtedly be regular conferences among the developing countries themselves to serve as a forum for fairly frank discussion of problems and requirements. The regional and international offices might sponsor the establishment of training facilities for personnel in the developing countries who themselves will become trainers with specific skills. Receiving ideas from people with wide international experience will give the country training officers a broader background and a richer fund of information and methods.

In this connection we might note the AID-sponsored Regional Training services that the Philippines has provided its neighboring countries. For seven years now our neighbors from Taiwan, Thailand and Indonesia, from Vietnam, Cambodia, Pakistan, and Laos have come to the Philippines to learn new skills in social and economic work, to benefit from our experience, and to take advantage of our institutions both public and private. As of last year, nearly two thousand have come to share whatever knowledge and skills we have acquired in the fields of agriculture and community development, health, education, and public administration.

Finally, there can be tremendous value in a program of international exchange of middle level manpower. This idea, which has come to fruition only in these last few years, offers great promise because it is the vehicle for something more than just the transfer of experience and skills from one land to another. It builds bonds between peoples as individuals and as nations that cannot help but contribute to international understanding and peace—which is, after all, the goal of all our efforts.

# MANPOWER PLANNING

### REVIEW OF CONFERENCE DISCUSSIONS

The several proposals for international exchange of experience made by Vice-President Pelaez are symptomatic of the many areas of this problem still inadequately explored. The massive, urgent effort now being put forward by national leaders around the world to raise living standards and to create opportunities for richer and fuller lives for their people—indeed, the whole economic development effort—has no precedent in human history. Without experience to guide us we still have to learn as we go along, to correct and profit by miscalculations, and to take into account relationships which we may not have noticed when we started.

Thus country after country has come to realize fairly recently that systematic, centralized, detailed examinations and projections of the condition of their human resources are an absolute requirement for economic growth. The point has been brought home sharply in repeated instances when well-considered national development programs have foundered for lack of trained manpower. A clearly defined manpower plan, realistically correlated with the economic development program itself and put into practice at the same time, is a precondition of forward movement.

It could be argued that the mere existence of more and better jobs in certain sectors of the economy will eventually produce the necessary supply of trained people to fill them. Over the long run, this may well be true. However, one of the dominant characteristics of the effort in which developing countries are engaged is urgency. Given the political, economic, and social pressures which are building in these countries, it is impossible to wait for the situation to right itself naturally. Left untouched, furthermore, the existing patterns actually intensify the problem by inhibiting or even crippling the establishment of enterprises which could otherwise be successful, and by perpetuating imbalances in the distribution of skills in the labor force. For example, Puerto Rico discovered early in its "Operation Bootstrap" that vocational schools were graduating hundreds of people for whom there were no jobs, equipping them with skills which were obsolete. And Oscar Palacios Herrera of Venezuela points out that his country, through inertia, continues to train types of middle level workers that are not needed for the development of the country. Moreover, he notes, "Our universities continue to produce lawyers and economists, as do other countries in Latin America, far in excess of the ability of the market to absorb them."

Failure to plan effectively for the development of skilled manpower at all levels will brake an economic development program for a number of years. As Pakistan's Zahirrudin Ahmed dramatically underscores in the preceding chapter, money can usually be found somewhere but human skills are another matter. Says the Indian Government paper cited earlier:

The education and training of men and women in key fields of development is a time-taking process. The degree course in Engineering takes 5 years in India, and in Medicine 6 years after completion of the Higher Secondary Course, and normally 2 years' practical training is needed after qualifying for the university degree. The training of middle level manpower such as technicians and skilled craftsmen also generally covers a period 1½ to 2 years after completion of general education up to the prescribed standard. The formulation of plans and policies and the setting up of additional educational and training facilities may also take 1½ to 2 years in most cases. The supply of scientific and technical manpower cannot thus be increased all of a sudden, and calls for a good deal of advance thinking and preparation.

While the main emphasis in the arguments for comprehensive manpower planning has been laid on the point that the national interest demands it, an equally compelling case can be made on the ground that the immediate interest of the individual citizen requires that manpower programs and economic progress move along in concert. While it is true that a country must have certain skills available if it is to progress, it is just as true that men and women in a modern society must have some kind of fundamental knowledge if they are to be productively employed. The tendency is to view the problem in overall, statistical, somewhat mechanistic terms, but the fact is that this is a very human dilemma indeed. We are talking about the need— even the demand—of men and women for a means of livelihood; and we have seen that large numbers of them are not going to get it unless their government institutes a formal manpower development program based on existing resources and future requirements.

But our thinking has now fairly well passed through the stage where the argument for integrated manpower planning has to be made; too much equipment has lain idle for lack of men who know how to run it, too many plants have never been built because the supporting skills to make them profitable were not available, and too many people have gone unemployed or underemployed because their knowledge was unwanted or their preparation for today's world inadequate. The discussion now turns on the questions of what to plan, what factors should be considered in planning, how one should go about it, and the pitfalls and limitations. Let us see where the collective experience of countries has brought us in these matters to date.

### What to Plan?

The conference record is not lacking in specific suggestions as to manpower areas which need to be planned. Obviously the supply and demand for manpower at all levels needs to be assessed, and methods of using existing resources and developing those that will be required by the changing, expanding economy have to be fashioned and implemented. This general statement can be clarified by some illustrations of the kind of activity which should be committed to blueprints.

For instance, the Government of Israel calls special attention to the educational system and the likelihood that it will need to be overhauled in many countries. Too often it is based on the patterns of former governing powers, and not well suited to supply current needs for middle level personnel. In a technical paper[1] prepared for the Conference, Israel describes its own efforts to devise a system of education which will fulfill the need for rapid industrialization and large population increase:

With free and compulsory primary education between the ages of 6 and 14, Israel has developed long and short term systems to supply its rapidly growing needs for middle level manpower. We have sec-

---

[1] Government of Israel, *Manpower Planning and the Training of Middle Level Personnel in the Technical Field*, Technical Paper No. 6, International Conference on Middle Level Manpower; Peace Corps, Washington, D.C. (1962).

ondary schools which prepare the student for academic studies, but in addition there is a network of some 60 vocational schools to train youngsters who have left primary school in some 26 vocations, among them electronics, motor mechanics, agro-mechanics, printing, agriculture, photography, home economics, etc., in three, four or five-year courses. The intake of these schools has trebled since 1956 and today some 12,500 students are being trained annually.

To train new immigrants—the majority coming from countries with no technological background—and other adults, some 20 centers have been established throughout the country where accelerated courses of six months to a year prepare them for employment. New methods are continuously tried out in these centers. A comprehensive system of agricultural extension work and regional training centers for farmers has been established, and instructors work on the spot in new villages to train settlers in the methods appropriate for their farming operations.

As industry expands and agriculture intensifies, so does the apprenticeship scheme. Legislation has been passed to allow for day school attendance to broaden existing apprenticeship schemes. Parallel to basic training in various skills and trades every effort is made to upgrade existing manpower, whether it be in a particular trade or special field. Evening courses are being offered by various organizations, including the trade unions [Histadrut—the Israel General Federation of Labor]. Institutes have been established to train foremen, vocational instructors, managers, nurses etc. The Productivity Institute promotes efficiency and productivity through various activities and is actively engaged in directing and organizing specialized courses.

But the needs extend beyond the middle level manpower and into the pressing requirements for scientists, for specialists of all kinds, and especially for teachers. What kinds of highly trained personnel do we need, and how can we gear our educational system to develop them? This question is a central one for the planners.

Formal education, of course, is only a part of the picture.

Governments must plan for short-range, accelerated training which will equip people with necessary primary skills and re-orient others whose training has become obsolete because of changing economic patterns. Public and private resources must both be brought to bear on this effort and must be coordinated.

Planners will be called upon to establish priorities as between different sectors of the society and of the economy in conformity with the nation's goals. For example Ethiopia is determined to emphasize education, and India has decided that democratic de-centralization of the government should be a prime objective of her development efforts. Part of any manpower plan must be an allocation of resources, and this distribution has to be decided in accord with goals such as these.

Each country has special problems which call for particular attention. Norway, for example, is seriously concerned over cer-tain geographical areas where development has been slower than in the rest of the country, and she is developing plans to meet the situation. In other nations particular industries need special handling, and in still others racial or religious groups call for tailored programs. Thus, even within the overall plan, governments will find they need sub-plans for specific segments of the society.

For many governments the early employment of existing workers, as well as the initiation of programs to produce new jobs for the great increases in the labor force expected in the near future, hold a high priority. Mass unemployment is a spec-ter whose political, social, and economic overtones make for extreme anxiety everywhere.

Pakistan and others, as noted heretofore, raise the matter of labor wastage as an area worthy of major concern. The use of high level people in middle level jobs because of a shortage of specific skills, the mal-employment of specialists of various kinds, the diversion of technicians in short supply into non-essential activities, the failure to utilize womanpower are all examples of wasted resources—examples, incidentally, which are not unknown in better developed societies.

Finally, the use of foreign experts—both volunteer and paid—and a program for progressively eliminating them should be a subject of careful scrutiny. These people are needed for the short term to fill gaps in specialties and to train teachers, but they should not be built into the structure of the new society. Where to use such outside personnel, where to get them, what kind of training they should have, and how can they work themselves out of a job most rapidly all should be thought out.

### What to Consider in Planning

Of the many factors which have to be considered in the development of a manpower plan, most of them are obvious. As we have already observed, the condition and quantity of existing manpower and predictions of future needs are the principal ingredients of any workable program.

However, the discussions show that there are several elements which might be overlooked and consequently are worth special mention. One is the local pattern of basic trends subtly at work to change the manpower picture. In Norway, for example, the relatively high postwar birth rate means that the age distribution of the work force is going to change. The number of agricultural workers has drastically declined since the 1940's, while employment in industry and service occupations has risen rapidly. Automation is bringing marked shifts in the nature of certain traditional jobs. New technology of all kinds means that the content of a number of positions will be different five years from now; the danger of rapid obsolescence of skills is a real one in many places. Social legislation, such as the extension of compulsory schooling, will have an impact on the nature of the work force and the economic conditions of many families.

Other countries point especially to the population increase

and the tidal wave of people moving from farm to city as basic forces which must be carefully evaluated and fed into manpower plans. The success of public health measures in increasing life expectancy, the change from moneylending to banking, from handicrafts to modern industry, from subsistence farming to large scale agriculture, from small to large consumer markets —all these need to be taken into account.

Perhaps most important of all are the attitude and the value structure of the people. We are talking here about the dissemination of knowledge, a process about which we have a great deal to learn. It is simple enough to set out a program calling for a predetermined number of physicists and accountants; it is quite another matter to find the people who are teachable in those specialties. For "teachability" includes the willingness to be taught, even the desire to learn how to do things differently and, presumably, better. If the census figures represent what is available to work with, so does the system of values of the people. Manpower plans which have not taken into careful account the limits and the potentials set by public attitudes and aspirations are built on sand. Some observers, in fact, urge that these parameters be determined first, including some calculations on how much change can be generated in what direction and how soon, and that the development plans be fitted into them. Traditionally we have looked at the supply of capital and tailored our development programs to that; perhaps we should look at the state of readiness of our people, not just in terms of the technical skills they possess but their probable degree of acceptance of change, and let this be our framework.

## The Mechanics of Planning

The first requirement in hammering out a manpower plan, according to a number of countries, is the establishment of a centralized agency in the manpower field. For, as we have seen, the supply and demand of manpower are woven into every part of a nation's present and future, yet this very fact may produce a diffusion of responsibility in the area which can only yield uncoordinated, fragmentary and inadequate results.

As Mr. Ahmed of Pakistan explains, "The first difficulty we experienced when we started attacking the manpower problem was the lack of any one agency to look after the various aspects of this problem. When there is nobody who is really studying a subject or has the responsibility for it, the area tends to be neglected. So our manpower planning suffered because we had no central organization working on it. Consequently we have set up a National Manpower Council, a high-powered inter-agency group representing the various departments and ministries concerned with manpower problems, to coordinate planning on an organized basis."

Similarly Mr. Warren Woodham,[2] Director of Jamaica's Manpower Research Unit, describes the situation that existed in Jamaica when its first formal development plan was launched:

"The nucleus of a manpower program existed in many agencies; but at best it was *ad hoc*, improvised and poorly coordinated. The Ministry of Labor had some responsibility for aspects of a manpower program through their operation of the local employment service and the apprenticeship program. The Ministry of Education was responsible for all institutional training (vocational guidance was introduced at a later stage). The Department of Statistics provided at that time most of the statistical information on the manpower situation. Their reports were published at different times to suit different readers. These were principally administrative reports; the needs of development planning were only a secondary consideration.

"It was necessary to draw the facets of this program together

---

2 Woodham, Warren, *Elements of a Manpower Program for a Developing Country: a Jamaican Case Study*, Technical Paper No. 7, International Conference on Middle Level Manpower; Peace Corps, Washington, D.C. (1962).

and establish an effective institution to maintain a continuing program of employment market information, since national economic and social plans are meaningless without detailed manpower information."

Having pulled together the responsibility for manpower planning into one unit, the next question that arises is the positioning of the new agency. As one would expect, there is usually some concern as to just where in the administrative machinery of government such an agency should be established. Jamaica found herself no exception. Some of the recognized functions of her Ministry of Labor could hardly be exercised effectively without the continuing examination that a manpower program could contribute. Yet many of the problems of the employment market, the shortage of specialized personnel, the low level of literacy, the large labor surplus and the lack of many skills among the unemployed were such that they were outside the immediate sphere of responsibility of a ministry of labor—or for that matter, any single ministry. Then too, there was the other argument: since manpower planning is (or at any rate should be) an integral part of planning for social and economic development, should it not be a function of the organization responsible for planning the economic development program itself? The Jamaicans thought so, and placed their manpower unit under the technical responsibility, at least, of their Director of Central Planning, where it has been working quite smoothly for several years now.

Obviously in each country the location of the manpower group within the governmental structure will depend upon the local circumstances. The missions of the established departments, personalities and political forces, the machinery for coordination already in existence, and a host of other factors will be involved in the decision. But the point is that it must be centrally positioned and lines of communication must be established with the interested offices in all parts of the government.

On one matter, everyone offering experience in this area seems to be in harmony: the absolute necessity of close integration with the economic planners. "However," suggests the Indian Government paper, "There may be certain advantages, especially in the initial stages of development, in preparing a manpower program . . . so as to bring out the significance and inter-relationship between different items of the program. . . . It may assist the people who are concerned with different aspects of the problem to understand their own role and responsibility in relation to those of other agencies concerned." India feels that spelling out clearly the contribution expected of each agency concerned, and its indispensable place in the whole fabric, may help to ensure that important issues are not overlooked or underemphasized as a result of disproportionate zeal or pressure on the part of individual agencies primarily interested in other aspects of the job.

But, India points out, where a national plan is formulated, the manpower development program must be finally integrated with the general plan. This proposition, asserted and reasserted constantly throughout the conference, is of course fundamental to the present discussion.

Developing the necessary facts on which to build a manpower plan is the first task of the group. These statistics must be both macro and micro: trends of population growth, gross population figures, education and income levels, general analyses of occupations (farm, professional, manufacturing, etc.)—all are needed. Beyond this, detailed information on skilled occupations, the educational and training requirements for each of them, the numbers and ages of people currently equipped in these fields, the existing training facilities and their output, and estimates of future needs under conditions of growth must be obtained. Comparable data from other countries can be helpful as a guide in this area, although conditions vary so much from nation to nation that such figures can have only limited value.

## 50 : THE HIDDEN FORCE

The appropriate occupational classifications for this data will have to be developed, though they can often be adapted from standard breakdowns. One specialist—Harold Goldstein of the U.S. Department of Labor—suggests[3] that since the purpose of the study is to provide information needed for the planning of education and training, the answers have to be expressed in terms of occupations or occupation groups for which separate educational or training provisions have to be made. Thus, large groups of vocations requiring low orders of skill, and for which workers can be trained in a minimum period on the job, require no differentiation for this purpose and may be considered as a group. On the other hand, precision may be required for scientific, technical, administrative, and crafts occupations which call for long periods of specialized education or training. Therefore, in any one industry it may be necessary to examine the occupational composition in terms of only a few dozen separate occupations or broad groups, although the occupational specialists would be able to discern hundreds of distinct occupations in the industry.

The precise format for the collection of this data should be worked out by the specialists for each country.[4] Suffice it to say here that broad categories will not prove sufficient for the kind of manpower plan which a developing nation will need.

From this point on, manpower planning becomes an integral part of the development program. It is true, as Jamaica's Mr. Woodham points out, that "economic development projects are seldom expressed in manpower terms. The important variables that are usually considered include the cost of projects, and the

3 Goldstein, Harold, *Occupational Composition in Various Economics in Different Levels of Development,* Technical Paper No. 16, International Conference on Middle Level Manpower; Peace Corps, Washington, D.C. (1962).
4 For much information on the technical details of manpower planning, beyond the intended scope of the general conference discussions, the reader is referred to the list of conference publications and the extensive bibliography given in the Appendix.

anticipated levels of output from certain expenditures on agriculture, manufacture or other services." When a government equips itself with a manpower agency and adequate statistics, this will no longer be true.

### The Limitations on Planning

Of course, a number of factors impose limitations on the ability of a government to plan successfully to meet its manpower needs. In the first place, gathering the statistics is no easy matter. Even in the more developed countries, the tools for collecting and analyzing data are often inadequate; as government after government has discovered, it is a complex and difficult job to pull together accurate figures.

Secondly, it is extremely hard to predict manpower needs in the face of rapid change. Businessmen find it nigh impossible to provide more than a "guesstimate" of their expected shortages twelve months in advance under the most stable of circumstances; under the conditions existing in many countries, they can give only the roughest calculations. Extrapolation of existing data in terms of planned growth in a particular industry, too, can turn up only crude statistics. Too many variables play upon all such prognostications.

The fact that manpower programs must be indigenous to each country, and often to each section or group in each country, makes planning enormously difficult. "No country can tell another country how that country should be developed," says Minister Surendra Kumar Dey of India. "In fact, maybe one of the main difficulties in the world has been that we have been trying to tell others a bit too much how they should behave, how they should develop."

In the same vein, Ambassador Bernahou Dinke of Ethiopia urges the more developed peoples to fit their proposals into the plans of the recipient nation. "For instance," he says, "if a country has given priority to its cultural development and is concentrating all its efforts in that field, it will appreciate outside assistance which helps realize this particular program, rather than building materials for a housing development. It is wrong to suppose that the developing countries should be like small birds waiting with open mouths for whatever food someone else chooses to put in their mouths."

If this is so between countries, it can also be so within countries. As has been pointed out before, the value systems, the aspirations, the cultural patterns of a people may provide real impetus—or a real block—to manpower plans. Providing incentives to move men and women in a desired direction, developing their motivations to do what someone else feels is best for them is no easy matter, as more than one planner has found out to his distress. Materialistic carrots do not work automatically; often they do not work at all. And the use of sticks may conflict with a government's philosophy or the political realities.

Given all these limitations and many more, manpower planning cannot be a one-shot operation. As Teodoro Moscoso of the United States says, "We must plan the middle manpower programs not just for a breakthrough but for continuous development over a period of many, many years." Consequently, manpower planning is an ongoing process; the plan itself is only a rough approximation or guide, to be updated, altered, changed and refined as experience is gained and as the development progresses. The machinery for accomplishing this continuing re-evaluation and adjustment must be an integral part of the total manpower program.

Why, some have asked, plan at all if the blueprint is such a fuzzy and inexact document? The answer is obvious: because a faulty program, so long as it includes mechanism for its continuing re-examination and readjustment, is far better than none at all. Because the development of a manpower program forces us to look at questions we would never otherwise consider. Because it reduces the chance of miscalculation and failure by some degree. Because it gives people some sense of direction and some rational guidance. And because, as we learn more and more about how to use this development tool, it will serve us more and more effectively in the effort to release people in their eternal struggle to be strong and free. We cannot afford to abandon the job merely because it is difficult.

# Chapter

# IV

# Training Manpower for a Fast-Changing World

We have spoken broadly of manpower planning—the necessity to formulate an overall program for the general upgrading of the skills of a nation of workers. But what does this imply for the worker himself, the human being to be changed?

In terms of specific action, just what does manpower planning mean to the Andean farmer, the Asian laborer, the African craftsman, the young student choosing his future work? Can he be changed? And if so, what are the requisite characteristics of a training process in a world that is moving toward new goals?

## FIVE PRINCIPLES

### W. WILLARD WIRTZ
*U.S. Secretary of Labor*

The presiding fact these days is the fact of unprecedented change; not change in the slow, evolutionary sense, by which it has been the thread of all history, but change as it is measured today in megatons of technological, political, social and economic explosion.

To the extent that men's minds can grasp the infinite we are generally aware of what science has done, almost suddenly, to the very meaning of time, distance, the world, the universe. And yet there is only very vague awareness—just enough to arouse fear of the unknown—of the effects of this scientific revolution upon the whole concept of man's work.

A job used to be, almost universally, something a man expected to do the rest of his life. Often he inherited it from his father, or his lifetime work was dictated for him by the accident of his birth near a particular field or mine or seacoast or mill. But now, in a short span of time, a man's work has become directly geared to the developments of a science he neither controls nor understands—and therefore fears.

Thus the creative necessity we face in framing the manpower policies of our nations places a dual demand upon us.

First, we must keep pace with the genius of science. Technology is an inexorable force. Every new device is going to be used. What it is not made to alter for the better it will alter for the worse. And technology will not wait. It offers the promise of man's fulfillment. We must bring to the architecture of manpower policy the degree of invention, the innovation, the ingenuity, the boldness which characterize today's phenomenal rate of scientific discovery.

But when the scientist discovers a new truth, when the designer completes a new device, his job is done. Our task is harder. We have the further responsibility to develop those programs which will safeguard the individual who may be adversely affected by a technological development which greatly benefits the community as a whole.

Beyond this there is the responsibility on us to respond, to persuade, to obtain consent. Our task is to overcome the force of inertia which is represented in men's desire as individuals for even the incomplete security they think the *status quo* gives them. The promise of a higher standard of living for a nation as a whole, even as it includes the prospect of an individual's sharing in that gain as a consumer, cannot be expected to persuade him to risk his present job in the enterprise—especially if his house is mortgaged and there is another baby on the way.

There can be only one attitude toward the explosive force of the change we face. To ignore it would be ignorance. To fear it would be cowardice. Nor is it enough to be willing to "adjust" to change, for that would inevitably mean falling further and further behind until the forces of scientific and technological change which promise man's deliverance become rather the forces of his destruction. Tomorrow belongs to those who face the fact of change honestly, squarely, eagerly, who go forward to meet change not as an enemy, but as an ally—who see change as an essential quality of growth, who see growth as the meaning of life and who believe firmly that the future is a good idea.

This will become our posture toward change only as we assert —and establish in fact—the essential principles of a manpower policy which guarantees the full right and ability of every man to work—not necessarily at what he expected to do, or at what he used to do, or is doing now, but at a job which has meaning both in its performance and its contribution to an enlarged meaning of life for all of the brotherhood of man.

The vital principles of such a policy all relate to the need for new, invigorated, and perhaps more pragmatic concepts of education and training. At the outset they give rise to five propositions which we may put forward as axioms.

First, *everyone can be trained.* Every man and woman— properly counseled, tested, and referred according to his or her talents and aspirations to a vocational training course carefully designed to meet occupational needs—can partake in a vocational training experience and can become endowed with a meaningful and viable skill.

The United States learned in the development of its Tennessee Valley program that men and women whose previous work experience had been primarily in the agricultural pursuits of their forefathers were readily adaptable to the work and discipline of modern industry. Between 1940 and 1960 the number of workers employed in manufacturing in the Tennessee Valley almost doubled, from half a million to nearly a million. Middle level manpower demand and supply increased almost 100 percent. Personal income during those twenty years rose by 508 percent. Here is tangible evidence of how adaptable a work force can be, given the opportunity which an expanding economy offers.

Again this experience has been confirmed in connection with the U.S. Area Redevelopment Act of 1961. Retraining programs have been worked out under this act in areas where a particularly high rate of unemployment was prevalent. Consistently it has been observed that even persons with limited formal education, and even those who had been unemployed for a considerable period of time, have been able successfully to complete training programs involving skills previously unfamiliar to them and to secure new jobs.

The second proposition is that *everyone needs to be retrained*. An accelerating technology brings with it obsolescence of skills up and down the occupational ladder. No longer is it possible to train for, enter, and then stay until retirement in one occupation without further training. Always new skills have to be learned, or old skills updated, if we are to have a responsive, flexible, adaptable manpower supply to meet the demands of the expanding economy.

Third, *training is needed everywhere*. Industry and business are becoming more mobile, with consequent, sometimes almost kaleidoscopic, change in the location of employment opportunities. Even as the earlier traditional factors of location, such as nearness to power and transportation, are becoming less decisive industry must, in view of increasing skill requirements, pay more attention to the manpower aspects of an area. Different geographic areas, in turn, are finding more and more that their economic development turns on the skills of their manpower resources.

Fourth, *training methods must be improved*. This is partly a matter of adjusting the techniques of teaching to today's accelerating requirements and new challenges. Increasing emphasis is being put on various recently developed devices such as programmed textbooks, automated teaching aids, motion pictures, television, visual displays, slides, and mockups. But in the whole of modern educational technology these useful devices are merely some new tools. Technology obviously includes such machinery and gadgets; but it also includes an attitude toward problems, as well as a method of solving them.

The problems we face in this world, whether they are those of the cold war, of the population explosion, unemployment or underemployment, industrialization, urbanization, automation —all these problems will be resolved intelligently only when a larger proportion of the world's citizenry receives more and better education and training.

And fifth, *those who do the training must be especially flexible and responsive to the changing conditions of the world of work*. The real measure of the success of our manpower policies and programs will be our ability to anticipate scientific and technological developments and to prepare for them in advance. To the extent that we accomplish this we will serve the essential purposes of (a) neutralizing the concerns of individual workers which now prompt them to hold back and of (b) eliminating the drag on economic development which follows from any shortage of needed skills and competence in manpower, especially middle level manpower.

Governor Luis Muñoz Marín of Puerto Rico, speaking of his

commonwealth's need to develop new economic institutions and strength, has wisely said:

Only by carrying the feeling of brotherhood to the modes and practical institutions of his life can man find his way out of the tragic blind alley into which he has got himself by permitting his science to develop more rapidly than his wisdom to guide its use. . . . The change that is in order is that of the attitude deeply understood through wisdom, vigorously clarified by intelligence, and severely judged and maintained by conscience. . . .

This economic objective (of increased production) is not only desirable in itself but is also a basis and means for a more tangible justice among men and a broader possibility for the enjoyment of cultural and spiritual values. . . . Nor does the forward march of technical development suffice, nor the skills of the workers, nor the know-how in all branches of production and marketing; even if we had all of these things . . . still one thing would be lacking. This is the stern and unflinching willingness to sustain a clear concept of priorities in regard to all the things we want to do and which have to be done to improve the living conditions of the people.

We will "sustain a clear concept of priorities" only as we recognize that "middle level manpower," "full employment," "expanding economy," are catch phrases for minor premises in the logic of life. The major premises are necessarily cast in terms not of institutional, but of individual interests. Our economics will be no less sound for taking counsel of social precepts, nor our proper respect for efficiency diminished in any way by due regard for human consequence.

Today, when it looks as though man is more in danger of becoming a robot than a slave, our attitude toward our economic objectives must be all the more vigorously clarified by intelligence, and severely judged and maintained by conscience. Surely those whose concern is about a current manpower shortage are already fully aware of the costly consequence of regarding labor only as a supply factor in the equation of a necessarily expanding economy. Labor is not a commodity.

A more subtle yet no less real danger, perhaps, is that some whose concern is with an apparent excess of manpower may conceive their goals in too narrow a sense. The temptation is to think of full employment as an end in itself. Yet if that were the end purpose, it could be served by reducing hours, curtailing productivity, or providing meaningless work. Such measures would raise the job total and, in some cases, the apparent gross national product. Yet they would leave the economy relatively stagnant, and, what is worse, they would waste the nation's essential manpower wealth.

President Kennedy has spoken of unemployment as "a paradox because it develops in the midst of vast unmet human needs." We know that the only true wealth of any nation lies in the capacity of its people to produce both ideas and things, and that we fail in our appointed task unless we use whatever may be our full manpower potential to meet people's unfilled needs.

The framing of manpower policies can have no ultimate validity except as part of the broader function of social architecture. No manpower policy is complete unless it is concerned equally with the man and with the power which he represents. Just as we have unlocked the power that lies in nature, so will we find full use for the power that lies in man. Surely the goal of all organized life is the emancipation of individual energies. If we can find ways to meet this need, we shall have found—to use Alexander Pope's phrase—the key to that drawer in which lie other keys.

## EDUCATION AND TRAINING

### REVIEW OF CONFERENCE DISCUSSIONS

In postulating his five basic principles—acceptable in themselves—what Secretary Wirtz leaves to be said by his international colleagues at San Juan is that for many developing countries there is the dilemma that the job is so big, so complicated by conflicting factors, that it is difficult to know where to begin. Shall the emphasis be placed on rapid, specific vocational training programs to get new productive enterprises in motion quickly, despite the difficulty of doing this with a population that in some cases is still hardly literate? Or is it more important to concentrate on raising the general educational level or at least the literacy rate, and so to open the gates of successful communication and full membership in today's developing community as a precondition for training in skills that will not stand still? Do we start with the chicken or the egg?

Under such conditions can we generalize from the experience of the developed nations in framing immediate manpower training policies for newly developing countries? State Council Vice-President Nicholas Pichardo of the Dominican Republic says no. To do so incautiously might bring great harm, he warns. It is true that in some degree all countries share the common problem of accelerating the supply of middle level skills, but the problem is very different in a country where the workers have already received a basic formal education.

Even in developing countries where literacy programs have made a start among the workers, "you can't consider them cultured simply because they can read," says Mr. Pichardo. "It would be dangerous to launch a tremendous mass of our fellow citizens into a purely technical education without that [cultural] basis. We feel that technical training to prepare the average worker should be carried out through governmental action of a fundamental type, to provide the workers with the necessary background to perfect their knowledge in the ethical and moral field as well, which will permit them to be men of integrity in the service of their country.

"We should also use the presence of this mass of workers in schools and educational institutions," he continues, "to correct three other troubles which at present impede the development of our countries. One is the laziness or apathy of our peoples; this is not innate, but is conditioned by hunger and lack of education. The second is social inertia—which we might describe more cruelly, perhaps, as social irresponsibility. It is essential that we educate our masses so that they will not expect everything to come from others more powerful or from the government, but will understand that they too have a duty to contribute to the progress and improvement of their communities. And third, in the field of personal will, is the matter of sexual education that can free us from the tremendous problem of overpopulation—a factor which threatens our development in a very real way."

Brazil's Flavio Amaro de Brito supports the thesis that middle level manpower training cannot be totally divorced from general education. "But on the other hand," he says, "a general or formal education demands considerable time and a combination of many efforts and resources, while training can be carried out with little resources in a shorter time and therefore remains outside the field of general education." Explaining that the two are conducted along separate paths in Brazil, with vocational training handled largely by industry itself, he voices his country's conviction that training programs should be oriented primarily to the requirements of the communities destined to benefit from them. "Training should not be carried on for its own sake, but in the light of need," he declares. "If it is not obeying demands of communities it may constitute a waste of effort."

Such a view is reflected in the United States Manpower Development and Training Act of 1962, although of course its special circumstances may find only a limited parallel in a newly developing country. Its purpose, as pointed out by U.S. Labor Secretary Wirtz, is the retraining at public expense of some 400,000 workers, chiefly in the middle level category and most of them victims of technological displacement. This act stresses training for specific community needs, and moreover is directly tied in with placement services. In other words, its specific training programs may be undertaken only when there is a reasonable expectation of appropriate jobs in the immediate future.

In much the same way, if less restricted, Italy's domestic vocational training programs are directed toward short-run objectives. With her substantial rate of industrial development Italy has had the heavy task of providing training for hundreds of thousands of workers, both in upgrading formerly unskilled labor and in retraining to keep pace with technological advances. Italy's spokesman Giuseppe Lupis, speaking of his country's nearly two thousand vocational training centers organized by the Ministry of Labor, observes that the program is designed mainly to furnish quick training in specified occupations.

But there are many who have reservations about such a course. A long-range approach is vital to a newly awakening country, believes Mondher Ben Ammar, Tunisian Secretary of State for Public Health and Social Affairs. "The economic development plan of Tunisia emphasizes the individual, not the worker," he says. France, too, is concerned about the ultimate wisdom and possible effects of training merely for narrow, momentary objectives. "Undoubtedly we are tempted, in view of the great tasks to be carried out, to initiate accelerated training," observes Jean Basdevant, Director General of the French Office of Cultural and Technical Affairs. "But from our own experience in this area we in France feel that its use must be tempered with caution. We believe that all modern training methods should be applied in the developing areas; yet we also believe that accelerated training—that is, very fast training—is not satisfactory for the countries we want to help. Certain countries in the East, after the war, tried to manufacture physicians in two or three years; they had to give it up and go back to normal methods of training. We believe every man in any country is a human being, and that training and education should be one and the same in whatever latitude it may be."

Actually most of the developing countries are attempting a combined approach, recognizing on the one hand that a general educational background must accompany vocational training if the necessary full potential of their workers is to be realized—yet on the other hand that the pressure for new production will not wait and that some emergency training, however incomplete and regrettable, is essential to meet the needs of immediate economic development projects. Thus the Israeli Government[1] says, "It takes over ten years to train a technician. At the same time short term projects must be undertaken even if this means adjusting the accepted standards and scope of each trade for the time being." The statements of many are similar.

Maidah Mamoudou, Minister of Education for Niger, goes a step further. "It is urgent," he says, "that Africa pursue training on the spot of all the personnel it needs. But in the meantime, the Peace Corps volunteers should be ready to fill in this gap in all the fields of national activity, education, public health, public works, etc." The same thought is offered by Sierra Leone's Minister of Education, Ahmad D. Wurie, who says, "If Peace Corps volunteers could be had to fill the middle grade posts while the people of the country are being trained, this would go a long way towards solving the problem."

---

[1] Government of Israel, *Manpower Planning and the Training of Middle Level Personnel in the Technical Field,* Technical Paper No. 14, International Conference on Middle Level Manpower; Peace Corps, Washington, D.C. (1962).

### Instant Manpower

Are the stop-gap measures of quick training actually in conflict with the more basic, long term educational need expressed by so many of the developing countries? Not if properly applied, feels Deputy U.S. A.I.D. Administrator Frank M. Coffin. "We cannot do the subject justice by approaching it only from a tactical viewpoint," he declares. "Now that we have instant orange juice and instant soda water, are we merely interested in using new techniques to turn out instant sub-professionals? Obviously not. We have new weapons which lend themselves to new tactics. But their best use will come from fitting them into strategic thinking about the development of a country's physical resources and the overall educational task of lifting the sights, opening the minds, and broadening the area of concern of the people of each country."

Nevertheless, instant manpower, or the nearest possible approach to it through modern accelerated training methods, is clearly one of the subjects uppermost in a good many minds. Mr. Coffin himself speaks of quick training programs that have successfully placed workers in new occupational employment within sixteen weeks. "This is not a substitute for education," he acknowledges, "but we are talking about a specific approach to a specific problem within this whole framework of economic development." He stresses the factor of vividness in new rapid training aids which appeal to the eyes and hands of the students as well as to his ears, and the value of techniques based on actual practical work as well as the classroom. Selectivity in subject matter also is emphasized. "Particularly for training middle level manpower," he says, "it is important to select things that need to be taught for that purpose and no more."

Along the same line Chief Minister G. F. L. Charles of St. Lucia lists some of the immediate needs of his country to speed up and maintain stability in the development process. These include more scientific aids to learning and teaching; school broadcasts and a general radio education program; pre-vocational courses at secondary school level in woodworking, science, education, and commercial secretarial work; on-the-job training in agriculture, community development, road building, carpentry, plumbing, and other vocational skills; and technical leadership training in the organization of on-the-job programs.

In the final analysis the argument of urgency appears likely to prevail. "The needs are very large and the time is relatively short," says Pakistan's Zahirrudin Ahmed. "For our own current five-year plan the numbers of people needing training, particularly in the middle manpower levels, are far in excess of what we actually expect to be able to add in our existing institutions or even through the institutions that we are planning. This underlines the importance of devising simplified techniques which can train people in a shorter time than usually taken under the present system."

The introduction of quick training aids appears to proceed most rapidly in the manpower programs sponsored by industrial enterprises, of which numerous illustrations from various countries are given in Chapter V. Presumably this is because an individual enterprise is in a position to define its immediate needs very narrowly and specifically. From this standpoint, as would be expected, the results in terms of early production increases can be very impressive; and as will be seen in Chapter V, quite a few developing countries are placing major reliance on this avenue of training.

Yet on a national scale, as one conference document[2] points out, both the timetable and the contents of the development plan should determine the extent to which a country relies upon

2 Fisher, Paul, *The Role of Middle Level Manpower in Social and Economic Development*, Technical Paper No. 6, International Conference on Middle Level Manpower; Peace Corps, Washington, D.C. (1962).

abbreviated specialized training, as against the more time-consuming general education expected to produce well-rounded craftsmen and citizens. Similar considerations must decide how much effort should be spent in improving the skill level of the presently employed, as against the need to prepare future middle level manpower generations through training and education.

### The Barrier of Tradition

Not the least of the manpower difficulties in a newly developing country are the persistent vestiges of old customs—old ways that belong to the semifeudal economy from which such countries are endeavoring to go to a progressive, modern economic system. Conference delegate Armando Endara of Ecuador sees this as one of the main problems in his country. Not only is there a holdover of old systems and methods in agricultural and industrial work, but Ecuador—like some other Andean countries—is struggling to incorporate into its active society some millions of indigenous Indian inhabitants who until now have been virtually outside the normal economy of the nation.

Speaking for the emerging nations as a whole Mr. Endara observes with candor, "One of the characteristics of developing countries is that their populations are not devoted to work. They are living satisfied and happy with the small means that they have. Therefore, it is the duty and task of the government . . . to reach and stimulate their minds, to acquaint them with the aspirations and hopes of modern civilization, and in this manner to educate them to improve their lot."

To be sure, this is just an unusually pronounced manifestation of the fairly general problem of shifting from a traditional, static subsistence economy. Yet it does raise the question, in some newly developing countries, of precisely where the middle level trainees are to come from until a rise in the general educational level alters the situation. Nigeria's Minister of Labor, Joseph Modupe Johnson, comments that most of his country's craftsmen such as blacksmiths, goldsmiths, and mechanics are still using old traditional methods, because of lack of technical education and modern machinery. These inherently capable individuals may furnish a likely reservoir of trainees for more modern production methods; but, as one study[3] points out, in quite a few countries such traditional craftsmen are immobilized in their fields by social custom (e.g., caste, etc.)

In these circumstances one suggested source is immigration. There are some countries, such as Italy, where surplus workers—even trained workers—have long been the rule rather than the exception, and which continue to train middle level manpower for export. Likewise, there are developing nations which have consciously employed immigration as a source, with or without pre-training. The Israeli Government notes that in its fourteen years of existence Israel has integrated, trained, and settled on the land or otherwise provided productive employment for more than a million immigrants, most of them from countries with little or no technological background.

### Other Special Hurdles

Practical experiences with manpower development programs in emerging economies disclose other special difficulties not always superficially apparent. For example, Bolivia's Minister of Public Health, Guillermo Jauregui Guachalla, indicates that in his country the present shortage of middle level technicians and skilled workers is aggravated by a constant exodus of such trained people to other countries offering better working conditions. Somewhat similar is the dilemma posed by Ahmad D.

3 Shapiro, T. R., Adams, W. and Gordon, J., *Labor Demand and Supply for Middle Level Occupations in Developing Countries*, Technical Paper No. 8, International Conference on Middle Level Manpower; Peace Corps, Washington, D.C. (1962).

Wurie of Sierra Leone, in that many young people sent abroad for training do not wish to return home with their new-found skill or, if they do return, often refuse to take up the work for which they have been trained. Actually this problem is fairly common among the developing areas. The young engineer is reluctant to give up the bright lights, the modern comforts, the satisfaction of up-to-date professional facilities that he has tasted during his overseas study period—especially if he feels that an outmoded scale of values at home still offers little enhanced status or compensation in his field of training, and that if he must return he can do better in his father's importing business or marry into a better dowry as a routine clerk in a government office.

No less perplexing is the difficulty noted by Nigeria, which now has five universities but not enough middle level technical institutes. Although the burden of vocational training is for the moment being shared by the universities, and by local industries which are currently carrying over two thousand apprentices, the country's needs are still not being met—partly, says her Minister of Labor, "because in view of the prestige and remuneration attached to those with university degrees, most of the students from secondary schools want to go on to university work irrespective of their abilities and financial standing." Recognizing the need for the government to build more vocational schools, he feels nevertheless that there must be school counselors to guide students into the paths of their individual capabilities.

With the need for counselors Edward Seaga of Jamaica agrees, although at a lower level of schooling the problem itself may actually be reversed. Jamaica, which spends proportionately more on education than do many other developing countries, finds that only 7.5 percent of persons leaving primary schools choose to pursue further education, thus considerably narrowing the stock from which the best trainee candidates for many middle level skilled occupations may be drawn.

Mr. Seaga recounts another unforseen problem in this category. When Jamaica organized an accelerated training program in building construction skills, intended for young men eighteen to twenty-five years of age, it was found that because of family obligations or other commitments most youths in this age group were more interested in a current job at any pay than in stopping work to be trained. On the other hand, those who did enroll—youngsters of fifteen or sixteen just out of school—afterward were found difficult to place in employment because of their age.

Many countries recognize the traditional resistance to diffusion of manual skills stemming from outmoded concepts of "face," but while this still exists in varying degree it is less of a problem than it used to be. In Malaya, for instance, much change has come about through constant reminders to the people of their participation in every aspect of national development. Says Malayan Ambassador Ong Yoke Lin, "The dignity of working with one's hands is highlighted, and the old prejudice or snob value of formal education tailored for white collar jobs is slowly dying out."

In its place, however, the possibility of a new psychological problem looms. Both Israel and The Netherlands note that under some conditions, after accelerated training, a man's vanity about his newly acquired knowledge may prevent a balanced relationship to his fellow craftsmen. Mrs. Golda Meir, Israel's Foreign Minister, suggests that this danger may be alleviated if the recipient of accelerated special training is made aware of its limitations and of his own need to fill in the theoretical background eventually. She proposes that such trainees should in due course be sent back to school, possibly during off-work hours, to acquire an educational foundation to the quick training already received. In this way some such trainees may become sufficiently qualified to teach others, moreover.

## On-the-Job Training

Some specialists[4],[5] doubt that formal training in vocational schools generally is as effective in preparing craftsmen as on-the-job programs and apprenticeships. It is also pointed out that industrial employers often reject the output of trade schools, preferring to hire workers of less preparation and do the training themselves. The trade schools are not infrequently behind the times; in other cases, the nature of their training may be inadequate to impart a genuine skill, yet the graduation certificate may convince the trainee prematurely that he is too far advanced for a practical apprenticeship and should at once receive a fully skilled worker's wage.

For these and other reasons, on-the-job training is strongly advocated by many of the countries participating in the San Juan Conference. Some, like Venezuela, Malaya, and Germany, prefer to place their major reliance in it as a basic means of skill diffusion; others bolster this view with their emphasis on the high cost of separate vocational schools, the limited number of instructors available, and the student's not infrequent need for income during his training period.[6]

Yet Thailand's Nai Boonchana Atthakor calls attention to the fact that a country in the early stages of development may find the merits of on-the-job training more hypothetical than real. "In Thailand," he says, "it is extremely difficult for people to acquire skills beyond minimal levels through actual work experience. Since productive techniques are not very advanced, apprenticeship training is not very popular. Formal education is therefore relied upon for the training of manpower in most occupational and professional fields." Others note also that

---

[4] Shapiro, T. R. et al., loc. cit.
[5] Fisher, Paul, loc. cit.
[6] Fein, Rashi, The Integration of Educational Planning with Economic and Social Planning, Technical Paper No. 9, International Conference on Middle Level Manpower; Peace Corps, Washington, D.C. (1962).

some on-the-job training may be so specifically tailored to the employer's requirements that it deprives the worker of occupational mobility and weakens his chances for promotion.

Thus Japan, Venezuela, and others refer to the importance of enough flexibility in vocational training methods and content to adjust to the constantly changing times. The Japanese Government sets standards for the curriculum, training period and other matters relating to vocational training within private firms or groups who operate cooperative vocational training programs. It also conducts tests designed to judge objectively the worker's skill in fifteen major trades. Japan's skill training is carried on both in firms and in public vocational schools, but in 1961 some 68,000 persons received on-the-job training while the schools trained 61,000.

### Swords and Plowshares

A large potential training area often overlooked, in the opinion of Israel's Mrs. Golda Meir, is the army. Faced with a necessity for universal compulsory military service of twenty-four to thirty months for youths over eighteen, Mrs. Meir says, "We feel that we cannot afford to waste two or more years of a young person's life merely in military training." Accordingly, Israel combines army service with vocational training. Whether in agricultural or industrial pursuits, metal work or electronics, teaching or nursing, this nation has seen to it that her young people leaving the army are better suited for a fruitful life and for a part in the national development effort. As a typical illustration, one special army formation devotes part of its time to agricultural training in villages; upon completion of their military service, its members are sufficiently skilled to be the core of a new agricultural village in a selected development area.

A similar program is being contemplated by Iran, according to U.S. Vice-President Lyndon Johnson. In this plan, it is understood, only a small part of each day would be taken up with physical exercises and military training. The rest of the time would be devoted to such work as road building and the development of the country's resources. Frank Coffin of the U.S. notes further that even for military needs all armies today must train a certain number in various specialties such as nursing, radio, mechanical and other work, and that some of the accelerated training methods developed by the U.S. armed forces may be adaptable in developing nations.

Many observe that agriculture must not be overlooked in discussing the needs for middle level skill training. While the national development process involves considerable stress on industry, transport, communications, and other aspects of a modern state, most emerging nations are still basically dependent on their agricultural sector and in any event will always have to feed their growing populations. In most cases, even the machinery for industrial growth must come through foreign exchange provided by the country's agriculture.

Vocational training in agriculture should cover much more than the proper growing of crops. Apart from the desirability of better educational background for the farm population—bringing the city to the farm, and so helping to check the unwarranted rush to cities—a modern farmer needs to know not only how to run a tractor but how to repair it.

However, warns David O. Hay, Australian High Commissioner to Canada, except in opening new and uninhabited lands there is no use in seeking "more and better farmers" if the actual trend today is to have *fewer* and better farmers. This is the inevitable consequence of more efficient farming, as the evidence of the developed areas clearly shows.

# Chapter

# Skill Development on the Job

"Private enterprise is the great university for the training of middle level manpower," declares Elias D. Lopez Ortega, Director of Venezuela's Institute of Educative Cooperation, in explaining his country's heavy reliance on this source today for accelerated skill training.

In much the same vein at least a dozen of the nations participating in the conference—both developed and developing countries—emphasize the essential role of the private sector in training the middle level manpower needed for national development. The discussions as well as the documentary contributions show general agreement among economic development authorities that the principal agencies of production—private industrial plants, commercial firms, and labor unions concerned with specialized skills—not only have a vested interest and a strong obligation to contribute to skilled manpower development and training, but in many cases are in the best position to do so effectively.

Here a fairly sharp distinction is drawn between the terms "education" and "training." It will be recalled from Chapter II that Dr. Heller, in making such a distinction, defines education as the process of developing basic mental ability and of schooling in the general knowledge which every citizen needs; training, by contrast, he characterizes as the teaching of specific occupational skills for particular kinds of jobs. One basis for the distinction is a comparison of the resulting direct and indirect economic and social benefits. Dr. Heller points out that education's overall or "neighborhood" benefit to a society so greatly exceeds the personal advantages gained by the individual being educated that it provides the traditional rationale for government support of education. "Society alone," he observes, "can pay for education in the measure of its total yield rather than its direct private gain."

On the other hand we have noted that skill training, because of its direct and perhaps large return to both the employee and the employer, can to a great extent be provided at private expense. This is not to say that there are no "third-party" external or overall social benefits from this form of training; indeed, accepting that manpower training is one of the key factors in economic development as a whole, it follows that its rewards are shared indirectly by the entire society. But an investment in specialized occupational training can more readily be justified in full, or nearly so, by an individual who expects thereby to gain a better income for himself, or by a commercial enterprise which requires the particular skills for viable production and will reap a satisfactory return on this investment in the form of profits from its immediately enhanced output.

As a prominent illustration Dr. Heller cites Italy, where a remarkably swift upgrading of the labor force has occurred, and where a very large proportion of the necessary training for this purpose has been provided, with obvious profit, by private industry. But the practice is fairly general, particularly in the developed nations, and as examples many others would serve as well. Further illustrations and useful experiences in this field are offered here by a number of the industrialized or more rapidly developing countries, including the United Kingdom, Puerto Rico, the Federal Republic of Germany, Switzerland, Sweden, Austria, The Netherlands, and the United States.

Britain's conference representative Dennis Vosper, in disclosing that some sixty thousand students from overseas are currently studying in the United Kingdom, estimates that among them are some nine thousand trainees from overseas private industries being trained by private industry in the U.K. Supporting the view of Dr. Heller and others, he voices Britain's belief that such training is not the task only of government but of private industry as well, and reports that many British industries are cooperating extensively with his government in this process.

In the training effort of Puerto Rico's well-known development program "Operation Bootstrap," the initiative admittedly has been largely governmental. But one of its former outstanding leaders, Teodoro Moscoso, now U.S. Coordinator for the Alliance for Progress, has this to say about its actual execution:

"One of the methods which we have found to be extremely useful in Puerto Rico, in the training of middle level manpower, is the full utilization of private enterprise in collaboration with government. This has made it possible to train people for specific jobs. The vocational schools themselves—which, by the way, are very expensive to run and can be quite a drag on the budget—have been enlisted to provide these trainees with some of the basic knowledge that they need. But at the same time they have been able to couple their programs to the specific requirements of individual industries, so that a trainee going to one of these schools knows that if he does well in his course there is a good job waiting for him. This has given a very fine motivation and has accelerated the training process."

Germany, whose own domestic needs have called for a great deal of accelerated vocational instruction because of the influx of some twelve million refugees and expatriates from East Germany and elsewhere, emphasizes training almost wholly through industry itself. Federal Minister Hans von Merkatz attributes this in part to the persisting vestiges of the common European handicraft traditions—modernized to be sure, but in origin dating from the Middle Ages. In any case, he points out, the German principle of vocational training is to depend to a lesser extent upon theoretical instruction and to lay stress upon learning through practical work. The responsibility of the trainee to learn quickly and to perform competently is intensified by making the training a part of the actual process of commercial production in Germany's factories and industrial enterprises.

The same principle has been extended to Germany's foreign aid in the training of middle level manpower. With the active support of its private industry, to date the Federal Republic of Germany has invited more than sixty thousand young trainees from developing countries for practical training courses of one to two years' duration in German industrial firms. The number of those presently being trained there is about eight thousand and steadily increasing. Significantly, Herr von Merkatz reports that only about fifteen hundred of these are currently having their training financed out of the federal budget and have come to Germany on government invitation. The other sixty-five hundred are classed as "nongovernmental" industrial trainees, the majority of whom have come to Germany on their own account or upon invitation of individual private German firms. But the contribution of the private sector in this instance goes even further than the actual vocational training. Cultural and social assistance to foreign trainees in their everyday life in Germany is provided by the Carl Duisberg Society—a private, nonprofit organization jointly supported by industrial enterprises, trade unions, and government.

## Influence of Export Market Forces

Swiss traditions in occupational training are similar. In this case there are some added reasons, and because of them the early industrial history of Switzerland offers features of special interest to students of developing countries. Here is a small state of limited natural resources, with a population of 5.4 million, which must import almost all of its raw materials and must export at least a third of its production (and 90 percent of its watches). Yet it is an industrialized country with a fully occupied labor force, and it is self-evident that this combination of circumstances can be maintained only through the best efforts in worker training. As of 1955 43 percent of its male and 14.5 percent of its female workers were classified as skilled labor, while the semiskilled category accounted for another 30.2 percent of the male and 52.6 percent of the female workers.

To acquire the necessary proficiency, a semiskilled Swiss worker is trained on the job. A typical skilled Swiss worker has passed a strict apprenticeship examination following three to four years of practical training in an appropriate firm, supplemented by compulsory courses in a vocational school. "Professional skill in our country is the product of a long historical process," Swiss observer Lukas Burckhardt explains. "It had to be learned the hard way. Out of necessity, merely to survive as an independent state under sometimes rather dangerous surrounding conditions, we have had to produce products of exportable quality."

It is not surprising, therefore, that in today's relationship with developing countries Switzerland has continued to emphasize professional education, and that its main impetus in overseas technical cooperation depends heavily upon private initiative, the government's role being largely one of coordination. In execution, too, the effort relies heavily upon private groups. For instance, the Swiss Foundation for Technical Assistance, which concentrates on school projects in developing countries for the training of apprentices in precision engineering and instrument manufacture, was set up and financed by private Swiss enterprise. Its current chairman is also president of the Swiss Machine Manufacturers Association, and the Foundation draws upon the broad overseas experience of this important branch of Swiss industry. Another private group, founded by persons connected with the chemical industry, is concerned with health service plans in Africa. Even the state-subsidized dairy farming assistance project in Nepal is under basically private sponsorship. Swiss machinery factories exporting their products to developing countries have established their own teams of skilled workers abroad, for installation and proper maintenance of the machines, and this results in further private industrial skill training on the spot.

Sweden, like Switzerland, feels a common bond with other small countries throughout the world—developed or developing —in the premise that any small country must produce first-class products if it is to hold its own these days and win a position in the world market. To this end Sweden's Minister to the United Nations, Mrs. Ulla Lindstrom, points out that Swedish vocational training, although voluntary, is founded on close cooperation between the state and local communities on the one hand and private enterprise on the other. Its basis is an "Educational Exchange" system in which the instruction of a trainee alternates between the school workshop and a specific place of work in industry. This keeps the school instruction closely geared to actual industrial production requirements, and adjusts the trainee realistically to modern working conditions and to the prevailing market demands of price-and-quality competition which must affect his output. An additional advantage of the exchange system is that training capacity is doubled when the same machinery and teachers can serve two groups of trainees simultaneously.

As an industrial country, Sweden has quite naturally taken a particular interest in the industrialization processes of the developing countries. Internally its training methods have proven so successful that in important respects they have been transferred to the Swedish training activities in other countries, and these technical assistance activities have especially centered upon the construction and operation of vocational schools.

In some of these Swedish overseas training projects, the desirable tie with actual production is achieved in special ways adjusted to meet local conditions. An example cited by Mrs. Lindstrom is the Swedish-Pakistani vocational school at Karachi. Here, with working capital provided by the Pakistan Government, a commercial production department for ready-made clothing has been attached directly to the school, giving the trainees practical experience in factory work, labor management, and business administration under strictly industrial conditions. This scheme makes it economically possible for the school to have available special-purpose machinery which would otherwise be too expensive to be amortized solely by a training school. The department's products are sold on a purely business basis, in straightforward fair market competition with the neighboring private enterprises in this same field of production.

Among other functions the production department of this school serves as a model establishment for those who would enter this business. It also subcontracts orders to private producers, particularly former trainees, who have started businesses of their own and still need advice and assistance. When necessary it may hire out machinery or do custom processing for such enterprises. To complete the picture an employment service for graduates is conducted by the school, and so far practically all trainees have been placed appropriately in the type of employment for which they have been trained.

The principle that vocational training should be combined with actual production experience within the country is one

which Sweden now tries to apply to all its overseas training activities. Apart from the work of vocational schools, a considerable amount of training is undertaken by the overseas
subsidiaries of Swedish firms. In a questioning of some thirty
large private Swedish undertakings having such training activities in 1951, all of them were of the opinion that strong economic and financial reasons favor training within the developing
country itself and in direct connection with the production
process. Sweden feels that the results of this policy are to a major
degree positive, and that its resulting overseas production is
generally operating at about the same standard as the average
in Europe.

One observation of Sweden from her own experience is that
highly automated production technique is not always desirable
in countries with an abundant supply of labor, where vocational
training is needed for as many as possible. Intentionally, therefore, the mechanical equipment used in these cases is not always of the latest type, and the training tends to be much more
all-around. There is particular emphasis on work supervision
and quality control, as necessary elements in countries which
have started to develop their industrial traditions only recently.
Equally stressed are the workers' social welfare facilities, as
another important factor in the development of efficient manpower.

In Austria, where special efforts have been made in the training of middle level manpower for developing countries, on-
the-job training within industry is closely connected with the
constantly expanding foreign trade activities of Austria's industrial enterprises. The Secretary-General of her Foreign Office,
Mr. Erich Bielka-Karltreu, estimates that about fifteen hundred
workers at the middle manpower level are now trained each
year in Austria's own industrial plants—the trainees coming
mainly from Afghanistan, Iran, Syria, Pakistan, the United Arab
Republic, India, Ethiopia, and Latin American countries. One

of the leading Austrian enterprises in the chemical industry established a training institute for agricultural extension workers in India in 1956, and for the Middle East it now maintains a similar advisory center in Beirut. Among other interesting approaches, one of Austria's largest steel corporations maintains a permanent team of ten experts who are sent upon request to developing countries for assistance in training.

### Dutch Enterprises Overseas

Efforts of the Netherlands in vocational training abroad are extensive, and rely particularly upon the Dutch private industries with overseas interests. Netherlands Technical Assistance Chairman Jan Meijer, summarizing their recent experience, points out that they have made highly effective use of new methods and techniques of training, some of which are undoubtedly more easily applied under the conditions of private employment. A critical selection of candidates, a thorough analysis of the job requirements so as to avoid superfluous subjects in the training, and a step-by-step presentation of the training program are among the elements proving effective in accelerating the training of unskilled labor or upgrading skilled people.

The Royal Dutch Shell group, now spending $7 million on training in developing countries, pay special attention to selection by means of aptitude testing. These tests are particularly designed to select, from a large unskilled labor force, those men who can best benefit from some form of apprenticeship or artisan training. Good progress is being made in developing reliable methods of selection suitable to large-scale application, notably in current experiments in certain African countries. The extent of this activity may be seen from the fact that the Shell group runs, in various countries, seventeen artisan schools and three technical schools, and has recently created a regional center serving Southeast Asia in the training for supervisory functions.

Some interesting experiences are reported by the Dutch electrical concern Phillips. Its training activity in developing countries originates largely in its sales organization, since successful selling of electrical instruments and appliances requires adequate provision for their upkeep and repair. An idea of the number of skilled people required for this type of servicing may be had from the 1961 estimate that in one European country the television receiver industry required 7½ million man-hours for production but six times as much, or 45 million man-hours, for service and maintenance.

In the developing countries Phillips recruits all such service personnel locally. It has devised new methods of training with some rather startling results. A two-month course now trains personnel capable of taking care of about 80 percent of the servicing work, including determining the reason for failure of the instruments and making the necessary repairs. The remaining 20 percent of more difficult repairs are handled by persons of somewhat higher technical qualifications, who are selected from among the ablest in the two-month course and given additional special training. Finally, the most outstanding of these receive still further training to qualify them as instructors for other locations. The number of persons trained in this way for servicing, as well as for skilled labor in assembly plants, is considerable.

On a more limited scale, interesting results in training highly skilled labor for toolmaking have been achieved for two new factories recently established by Dutch interests to manufacture precision instruments in India and Mexico. The production of these plants must, of course, meet the same standard of precision as that of the mother plant. A totally new approach in training by the use of modern accelerated techniques has made it possible, within a period of six months, to bring persons with a very limited elementary education up to the rather high technical level required for this type of production. Heretofore, in the Dutch tool factory itself, the normal training program for young workers has called for six years of general primary school education, three years of technical training at the company school, and two more years of training at the factory.

Citing such examples to show the relative weight given to training in the private sector and the rapid strides possible through this means, the Netherlands representative predicts a progressive extension of training activity in this sector as a consequence of increasing foreign investment and industrialization in the developing countries. At the same time he warns that today's remarkable new methods of accelerated training for very specific jobs are not without their inherent dangers, for of course every private industry is inclined to look at training solely in relation to its own needs. It remains the responsibility of government to keep the labor market under constant review, he points out, as both the economic situation and constant technological advance may create rapid changes in the demand for skills. In the Netherlands Antilles, for instance, the automation of the oil refineries entailed unemployment and a rather painful process of adaptation.

## Skill Development Through Foreign Investment

Where foreign private investment capital is sought by the developing countries as one of the important tools for economic growth, it is usual to think of it primarily in terms of its financial assistance and its commonly associated import of management technology. Less appreciated, perhaps, is the very real extent to which foreign and mixed capital enterprises can, and for the most part do, contribute directly to the local development of skilled manpower resources.

In generations past some countries have felt that such foreign enterprises were remiss in this field. But whether just or unjust in specific instances in earlier decades, the charge is seldom valid today. Much more has been learned about the economic development process. Since the two world wars, particularly, the attitude of foreign private capital has been increasingly one of a community of interest with the host country, of a mutual interest in the assistance and training of local skills and management techniques, and in the increasing assumption of operating responsibilities by nationals. As the conference discussions show, it is now widely recognized in many of the developing nations that foreign companies are playing a role of growing importance in the creation and upgrading of middle level manpower skills as well as those of the higher levels of competence, all so necessary to the social and economic progress of these countries.

Impressive illustrations of this function at work, as cited in turn by the San Juan delegates of numerous investing countries, have been reviewed throughout this chapter. To contribute similarly from recent experiences of the United States the conference secretariat, in preparation for the San Juan discussions, evaluated and reported[1] on the overseas training activities of a dozen major American firms operating abroad in as many different lines of commercial endeavor. The companies chosen for examination were not exceptional, but fairly representative of the better-known U.S. firms having significant foreign operations in the same and comparable fields of economic activity.

The chief differences among these selected firms are to be found in their businesses, which encompass such diverse lines as agricultural and other heavy equipment; office machines and computers; electrical appliances and industrial power equipment from light bulbs to large generators and turbines; motor cars and trucks; oil exploration, production, refining and marketing; pharmaceuticals; sewing machines and household appliances; varied agricultural and industrial production; ex-

---

1 Harary, Joseph A., *Manpower Training by Private American Companies Abroad*, Technical Paper No. 21, International Conference on Middle Level Manpower; Peace Corps, Washington, D.C. (1962).

port-import wholesale and retail distribution; retail chain stores; air transportation; and banking. In size, individually their annual volume of business ranges from a few million dollars to a billion or more. Their foreign operations vary in extent from a few thousand employees upward, the twelve companies together employing in their overseas work a total of about 575,000 persons.

It is interesting to note, first of all, that today less than one percent of these employees are U.S. citizens or expatriates. Even some of these few are merely trainees from the home offices sent abroad to become familiar with the overseas operations, and do not therefore displace any nationals. And while the number of nationals employed by these companies has risen constantly since the end of World War II, that of their American employees in foreign lands has continually declined through their replacement by nationals who were given the appropriate training.

Typically, one company, with 25,000 employees in Latin America, in 1956 had 500 U.S. and other expatriates, half of whom have been replaced by nationals in the last five years. Another company employing more than 100,000 abroad has among them only 900 from the United States, and in the last decade has reduced its Americans in Indonesia by nearly four-fifths. Still another has replaced all its American employees by nationals in Latin America, where its payroll numbers 2,000, and elsewhere now employs only ten U.S. citizens out of 1,800 employees. Figures of the others are comparable.

The company training programs that have made these changes possible are conducted under a variety of systems and combinations of methods, depending upon the skills to be developed. They include the maintenance or financing of full-time vocational schools and training centers, assistance to local public training institutions, operation of correspondence schools, on-the-job training schemes, the use of field groups from the home office to train local instructors, provision of special courses at the place of work (one of the larger companies had more than a hundred courses going on simultaneously during a recent average six-month period), and the sending of selected employees for training at the head office of other company operations, local or overseas universities, or the plants of machinery suppliers. The time devoted to training for specific skills varies from a few days or weeks up to as much as three years, and the courses range from the use of simple hand tools to special seminars for top management executives.

Already the consequences of these programs for the developing countries concerned are far-reaching, and go beyond the mere replacement of expatriate workers by nationals. Thousands of non-American employees now occupy supervisory and managerial positions, some in the topmost echelons of the companies. Practically all started at low levels, often as manual workers, and were promoted to more responsible posts as their capabilities were developed through training.

### Demonstrative Results

Some random examples tell the story. In one of these companies, which built a two-hundred-mile oil pipeline in Indonesia, at first all the key positions were necessarily held by Americans; now the whole operation is in the hands of Indonesian employees. Out of 900 supervisory positions in another company, 650 are now occupied by nationals. Still another has replaced 350 U.S. supervisory and professional employees by suitably trained nationals in a five-year period.

Virtually all the manufacturing operations of an electric light bulb factory in Turkey are now carried on by some 250 trained Turkish women, the majority of whom were formerly illiterate and unskilled. In scores of countries the branch managers of one of the largest American airlines are local citizens, all of whom have risen from lower levels through company training. The same is true of all the general managers of another firm having manufacturing and sales operations in seventeen Latin American countries. Many of the managers of the foreign stores of a large American retail chain are now local nationals, and their number is increasing.

The training has also had its impact on the size and nature of the local production itself. For instance, several of the American companies discussed here started their operations abroad in the form of comparatively small assembly plants. They were later changed to manufacturing plants with practically all component parts produced locally, as a result of the training given to a much enlarged labor force in their employ. The number of local workers in a Brazilian plant of one of the companies jumped from six hundred to nearly four thousand in a five-year period.

Many of the companies do not restrict their educational and training efforts to their own employees, but extend it to their families and dependents and in some cases even more generally as a public service to the country in which they operate. One American firm established vocational schools in Venezuela which it later gave to the government at no cost, and also opened its own training facilities to the employees of other firms both domestic and foreign. Another built, equipped, and operated a vocational school in Indonesia, later turning it over to the Indonesian authorities for use by the general public.

Several companies offer a substantial number of scholarships to local students for education in local institutions and American universities. One of these firms has financed U.S. postgraduate studies for about five thousand foreign engineers since World War I, all of them non-employees, and none of the engineers have been obligated to work for the company after completing their studies. In Brazil several American firms regularly take in groups of local students chosen by Brazil's own universities, giving them three to six weeks of on-the-job training in their plants, during which the firms pay them stipends without obligation as to where they use their training later.

Quite a few of the companies offer training to employees of their customers, dealers, and suppliers. An American bank finances each year special trips to the United States for some of its foreign employees, but even more for foreign bankers and government officials who attend a variety of seminars on banking and finance while observing operations in the United States. This bank also trains many employees of its foreign correspondents.

Thousands of foreign employees trained by American companies have later moved to other key jobs in private industry or in their local governments. Some have opened their own businesses. One company trained more than two hundred Turkish Government engineers and more than four hundred foremen and repairmen in the use, maintenance, and repair of heavy equipment, at a nominal cost to the Turkish Government which was far below the company's actual expenditure; the training lasted nine months and was done in a special facility near Ankara, erected by the local authorities. In one Latin American country the majority of the staff of its Ministry of Mines, when established, were former trained employees of one of the American companies.

These illustrations are but a few of the many practical demonstrations that the role of foreign private companies in creating and upgrading skills in the developing countries is a big one. Today's tendency, moreover, is toward an ever-increasing contribution of such companies to the social and economic progress of their host countries in the fields where the manpower shortage is most acute. The reason for the trend, clearly enough, is the convincing object lesson that such efforts benefit the companies themselves no less than the countries where they work.

### Encouragement of Private Sector Training

Up to this point most of what has just been said on this subject has come from the more advanced countries. Actually the importance of vocational training efforts through the private industrial sector is voiced equally by spokesmen of the developing countries, but with a slight difference. Typical of their current thinking is the statement by Mr. Zahirrudin Ahmed of Pakistan's Finance Ministry:

"One of the difficulties we have experienced is that of mobilizing the resources of the private sector in helping towards the achievement of higher technical skills among the people. We recognize that the greatest employer of new middle level manpower is going to be private industry and private business. Yet business and industry in our country have shown some reluctance, or at least inertia, in trying to meet these needs by launching training programs.

"As long ago as 1955 we started a voluntary system of private industry training, but nothing much came of it; private industry did not respond to the extent we had earlier expected. Now, more or less out of desperation, our government has sought a law to force private industry to help train the people it needs. To make this easier for them, however, we have supported the view that the cost of training is logically an ordinary deductible business expense."

Brazil's Flavio Amaro de Brito affirms the view of his country that the training of manpower, and particularly industrial manpower, should where possible be directly linked to productive activities; that is, the training preferably should be of the on-the-job variety, within the productive enterprise. He suggests the establishment within each country of a national training fund, supported through the participation of the enterprises and organizations which stand to benefit ultimately from the training. To offset the financial contributions of such enterprises he proposes to exempt them from a small percentage of their income tax, and to augment the training fund with a government contribution as well. In a sense Brazil is already experimenting along this line, in the operations of its Northeast Regional Development Institution known as SUDENE. The law establishing this institution already allows it to grant, for training purposes, an additional 3 percent in the amounts of loans to new enterprises established in the region, and further recommendations are being prepared to allow such enterprises an income tax deduction for the costs of worker training.

Edward Seaga of Jamaica supports the concept that where necessary developing countries should provide local industry with tax incentives for the apprenticeship and training of young people in the skills needed for industrial progress. Endorsing Mr. Moscoso's observation from Puerto Rican experience, he emphasizes that to institute vocational training schools requires a considerable capital outlay, whether by industry or by government. To the possible objection that a tax deduction for this purpose could mean a loss of government operating revenue, its prompt recovery through a broadened industrial tax base is implied in some figures furnished in another connection by U.S. Economic Adviser Walter Heller. In relation to the loss of gross national product due to unemployment, Dr. Heller estimates that if the United States unemployment figure moved from 5.8 to 4 percent of the labor force under present conditions, it would result in $30 billion more output.

The problem of encouraging private employers to train workers may arise out of various causes and cannot be related only to the country's stage of development. Norway's Kalmar Oksnes reports that on-the-job training programs of individual concerns in that country have declined because of the economic burden the apprenticeship time of the trainee places upon the employer. This tendency has been especially strong since 1950, and the Norwegian government has introduced a number of measures to make apprenticeship programs more attractive to industry. For example, there is now a system of government subsidies to employers based on the number of trainees accepted.

Norway also finds that it is not enough to offer vocational training of the proper quality and quantity: individuals must also be motivated to undertake the training best suited to their interests and abilities. The goal of the right man in the right job cannot be achieved without both occupational guidance and employment exchange service. Efforts are being made to incorporate vocational guidance as a part of the primary school training during the last three of the nine years of school, and also to have the student spend some weeks in an actual industrial enterprise or an appropriate place of work to acquaint him with working conditions and what is expected of him.

### Cooperative Training Schemes

Venezuela's National Institute of Educative Cooperation, INCE, operates not only through government but with joint participation of private organizations and labor representatives. This institution is devoted to skill training at all levels, for agricultural work as well as for the commercial and industrial sector. The key to its effort is given in the words of its director, quoted at the opening of this chapter, to the effect that Venezuela considers private enterprise the major source to be tapped for the training of middle level manpower. Accordingly, INCE tries to take advantage of the existing potential within each company, and especially to select and assist in preparing the most qualified technicians of each enterprise to serve as company instructors for the training of others.

The scheme involved has been developed with the assistance of the International Labor Organization. It begins in each case with a complete analysis of the specific field of training. Through instruction given after his regular working hours in a period of about two weeks, the selected and already qualified worker learns how to teach the type of work that he already knows how to do. He is shown how to write his own training manuals, and how to prepare training programs to instruct other co-workers. He then becomes the instrument for the training of further middle level manpower within his own company, or possibly in other companies in the same or different areas.

According to reports the program has shown considerable success in its first eighteen months. The system is very flexible and can be applied to other sectors of the economy. INCE has already acquired some experience in its adaptation to agriculture, especially in cattle raising and dairying, and in such important fields as agricultural mechanics. The program in the rural areas has been extended now to train workers in such matters as how to build their own houses, and how to apply modern trades to the rural conditions in which they live and work.

In Chile, while the state takes responsibility for higher education through the formal courses of universities and industrial schools, these institutions are also assisting in accelerated specialized training through centers coordinated with such agencies as ILO, foreign universities, and private enterprise. But a still closer tie with private enterprise is found in the training activities of the National Development Corporation. This organization—the Corporación de Fomento de la Producción—has established a special department responsible for the training of skilled manpower and middle level supervisory personnel. Its work is carried out both through the training of adult workers in special centers and by the training of personnel within industries themselves. Needs and priorities have been determined with the aid of an occupational survey of these categories of workers in Chilean industry, conducted with the advice of the ILO.

"However," says Chile's Minister of Labor Hugo Galvez

Gajardo, "all this work of the state, the international agencies and private enterprise towards the training and improvement of manpower is insufficient, and many years will have to elapse before its results become significant. . . . Our experience shows that even when the efforts of the national and international organizations are large, it is impossible to prepare the amount of middle level manpower demanded by our rapid transformation."

Possibly one clue to this situation is to be found in the observation of Mr. Dennis Vosper of the United Kingdom, that in recent years many countries have tended to concentrate on the devolpment of high-level educational institutions such as universities—no doubt, among other reasons, for their undeniable prestige value. Mr. Vosper suggests that perhaps as a general proposition this tendency has caused neglect in the parallel development of adequate technical institutes and middle level training institutions. Yet precisely this latter development, he feels, is the sort of thing that must be undertaken in the developing countries, and for which the more developed countries must provide instructors.

For this purpose the United Kingdom has recently set up a committee on Technical Education and Training for Overseas Countries (TEATOC), with membership drawn equally from U.K. educational authorities and industry. This is a very powerful committee, charged with the general development of this type of training and particularly with assisting in the provision of instructors and institutions overseas. One thing that is hoped from this new body is that it will be able to overcome a problem of which the United Kingdom has been conscious for some years: that so many of the students who come to the U.K. take their courses purely in educational institutions, and do not always get the desirable practical training in industry before they return home. But above all it is hoped that as much as possible of this training will be decentralized overseas, through the development of local institutions and training facilities within the countries where the manpower is needed.

### Private International Cooperation

On how private business and manufacturing enterprises of industrial countries can further help the private industrial sector of the developing countries, Mr. Vicente R. Jayme, Vice President of the Philippine National Bank, points out that there are many difficulties faced by individual industrial firms in developing countries which cannot normally be solved through the channels of institutional assistance provided by international and government agencies. A good part of these problems lie in the area of production efficiency, skill training, and middle level management, in which the local manufacturers themselves feel that the help needed for most effective improvement of their operations is the type they could best get in each case from another private industrial firm in one of the more developed countries. This is the situation disclosed by a survey of Philippine industries, says Mr. Jayme, but unfortunately in their poor financial position these enterprises are unable to meet the cost of such help, and in any event the appropriate private firms of the industrial countries are not always able to spare the necessary people to assist them.

Problems of this kind may very well receive some attention from a new voluntary program launched by an important segment of American business and industry, and announced to the San Juan Conference by U.S. Vice-President Lyndon B. Johnson. Under this program some of the leading U.S. enterprises have established a special committee within the Business Council for International Understanding, to study training needs in selected countries and to work with local industry and local government to help meet these needs. Beyond this step, the new committee will develop special programs for training nonemployee nationals, by methods ranging from expanded on-the-job training to various types of scholarships and grants.

### The Contribution of Trade Unions

One of the basic technical documents prepared for the San Juan Conference provides a searching examination of the trade unions' role—present or potential—in developing the manpower skills needed for economic growth.[2] It is recognized that these organizations constitute a natural concentration of skills, and that their greatest strength lies precisely in those areas of middle level trades, skills, leadership, and supervision where manpower development is most urgently needed in so many countries. Historically, skill training was, in fact, the purpose behind the original establishment of trade unions as craft guilds in the Middle Ages, although in recent times an increasing percentage of the responsibility for this vital function has tended, either by default or for various other reasons, to shift to the employer and to government.

The ever-present prospect that some competent trade union members may resent larger numbers of new workers being taught their skills, and so in theory diluting their power position, is outweighed by their own personal stake in national economic development as a whole, and by universal awareness of the serious scarcity of skilled workers to meet the development needs. Most often, indeed, the growth on which the future advancement of an individual trade union member must depend can come only through an increased supply of workers with similar skills. Thus, it is in the interest of the trade unions, as

---

2 Zack, Arnold M., *Trade Unions and the Development of Middle Level Manpower*, Technical Paper No. 3, International Conference on Middle Level Manpower; Peace Corps, Washington, D.C. (1962). The present text has drawn freely upon this publication.

already recognized by many of them, to make the great contribution that is in their power toward alleviation of the general manpower training problem.

There are those who may claim that trade unions constitute a hindrance to economic development by virtue of their pressures for higher income at the expense of increases in the national rate of investment, and that their interference with production through strike activities discourages foreign investment in the developing country. Recent studies have suggested otherwise, however. It has been pointed out that severe restrictions on consumption are required only during the initial stages of industrialization; that unions in developing countries are, in fact, too weak to make an appreciable impact upon either wage rates or investment; that their demands are largely to restore real income lost through progressive inflation; and that where they seek advances through legislation, generally such legislation merely codifies prevalent wage rates or extends fringe benefits with no real impact upon capital formation. In any event it is obvious that they have an identity of interest with the productive enterprises that must provide their employment and their reason for being.

Educational activities of trade unions today range from literacy programs to vocational skill training and leadership courses. Their literacy programs, particularly in the developing countries, not only help to overcome a general shortage of educational facilities but can be invaluable to the worker who has been forced by economic circumstances to join the labor force prematurely when he might have been in school. Of necessity such programs are less ambitious than those of government aimed at universal literacy. Yet they have the advantage of reaching selectively those individuals who have already demonstrated a certain drive by abandoning the traditional subsistence sectors of the economy for productive wage employment. In this sense they may sometimes prove more quickly rewarding, from the development aspect, than a similar effort toward universal literacy; for the trade union member, once literate, almost surely becomes a candidate for the more advanced training programs aimed at meeting middle manpower needs.

It is here, in the area of skill training, that the trade unions are offered their most challenging role in the developing countries. On the international scene there are already several working examples of what they can do with their unusual vocational training potential. One of the best known, perhaps, is the current training in building construction skills by the International Confederation of Free Trade Unions in Algeria. A similar program is developing in Kenya under the sponsorship of the Israeli Histadrut with the cooperation of the Kenya Foundation of Labor, not only in construction skills but in the operation of consumer cooperatives as well. Another is being conducted in New York City by the International Ladies Garment Workers Union, training African trade unionists in job skills and union administration. The Austrian Federation of Trade Unions is now preparing a training institute for an enrollment of about two hundred young Africans, to be trained in specialized industrial skills and handicraft work.

With such a promising start, it is not unreasonable to expect that such union-sponsored programs will expand in size and number as resources become available, as more individual unions become aware of their potential contribution, and as they appreciate the ultimate benefits to themselves that can result from such programs in the emerging nations.

Chapter

# VI

## Volunteer Service as a Development Instrument

From the San Juan Conference discussions reviewed to this point there is no mistaking the growing consensus that economic development is not a "spectator sport," to be played by a chosen professional team of government officials and large private investors while the rest of the population looks on from the sidelines and waits for the goals to be scored in their behalf. Everyone must play. The discussions leave little doubt as to the need for proportionately greater investment in human resources, for more intensive planning of manpower development, and especially for greater and more directly effective efforts by all sectors of the economy in expanding and upgrading middle level skills.

Meanwhile, for the most immediate development objectives can the process be speeded up? Is there any special catalyst available which could hasten this important work? Many of the San Juan participants think so. One of these is Sargent Shriver, Director of the United States Peace Corps, the organization whose global experiment with volunteer service as an instrument for aiding and developing human resources in the emerging nations is of interest everywhere. Mr. Shriver recounts the birth and early experience of the Peace Corps, and what it is trying to do today:

## THE FIRST YEAR OF THE PEACE CORPS

SARGENT SHRIVER
*Director, U.S. Peace Corps*

American astronaut John Glenn recently said, "As space and space technology grow . . . and become more ambitious, we shall be relying more and more on international teamwork. We have an infinite amount to learn both from nature and from each other. We devoutly hope that we will be able to learn together and work together in peace."

These are hopes that must be realized on earth no less than in outer space. As nations probe the infinite expanse of the universe, they must not neglect those expanses on earth which separate the strong from the weak and the rich from the poor. The development of nations is the process of developing men— a process in which, likewise, we have an infinite amount to learn from nature and from each other.

The Peace Corps is part of this process. As an enterprise it is working, not only because the United States has undertaken a major effort to make it work, but primarily because the people of host nations *want* it to work. They have helped it to work from the beginning. It is these host nations that are providing the momentum for an accelerating Peace Corps that today has almost four thousand volunteers[1] working in forty countries—

---

[1] As of October, 1962.

and will have some ten thousand in fifty-three countries by this time next year. As its contribution grows throughout the world, we see in it a symbol of renewed hope for our common destiny.

The Peace Corps was not a new concept. Voluntary agencies and private organizations had been engaged in similar activities for generations. But if the basic concept was not new, at least this was possibly the first time any government had decided to enlist the energy and talents of all its people on a national scale in such a service of peace and understanding. When he proposed the Peace Corps and asked for volunteers, President Kennedy was seeking Americans who would offer themselves, on a voluntary basis, for demanding tasks abroad—without conscription, at low wages, under new conditions, performing difficult work, waiving the usual diplomatic privileges and immunities, getting along without the usual trappings and trimmings of those who serve abroad.

The President's proposal was both timely and responsive. It came at a time when large numbers of individual Americans were seriously asking themselves: "Is there not some way I can make a personal contribution to better understanding among peoples, and to world peace?" It came at a time when millions of people everywhere had determined to share in the fruits of the modern age. It was a response to a world need, characterized by an African leader who said, "Africa desires to be understood and to be recognized from the viewpoint and perspective of her own people." It was a response to Gandhi's dictum that "isolated independence is not the goal; it is voluntary interdependence, law by nature and love, friendship, work, progress, and security in creative interdependency." It was a response to the belief that dedicated and disciplined individuals can illuminate the shared dreams of the human heart.

We all recall how the proposal of the Peace Corps brought the cynics to their feet. "It can't be done!" they argued. They dismissed it as a romantic idea, impossible of practical fulfillment.

At the Peace Corps headquarters, too, we shared many of the worries that bothered the critics, and we had a few more of our own. We remembered an African proverb: "Until you have crossed the river, don't insult the crocodile's mouth." Our river at that time was full of crocodiles, so we started by asking ourselves some fundamental, hard questions.

*Did foreign countries really want Peace Corps Volunteers?* To find out, some of us made a trip around the world. The answer was unmistakable. Everywhere we were deluged with requests for thousands of volunteers to teach in classrooms, to work in fields, to survey roads, to design bridges, to teach athletics, to do scores of jobs essential in a developing economy.

The second big question was: *Would enough Americans of high quality volunteer to serve?* In the first year, 30,000 Americans volunteered for the Peace Corps. We are now getting four times as many as at the same period last year and ten times as many general inquiries through the mails. Typically, in one recent week alone we received 859 applications. The quality of these new applications has remained high—higher in some categories than last year. The latest quarterly Peace Corps Placement Test, in September, 1962, was taken by 4,101 applicants, the largest number in the history of the Peace Corps. Instead of waning in the public consciousness, therefore, the Peace Corps has more ardent applicants than ever—despite the long hours, the low wages, and the demanding tasks!

A third question faced us: *Could we select the best qualified applicants for service abroad on a scientific, nondiscriminatory basis which would assure success to each individual?* All of us were conscious of this problem. Early in the history of the Peace Corps one Member of Congress said, "Mr. Shriver, I don't care if 100,000 people apply. Just tell me how you are going to be sure that you only send the best of them overseas."

For this purpose we turned to outstanding psychologists to set up a selection system that would produce the best qualified volunteers. The application blank itself is a difficult barrier to a capricious applicant. Some people say it's harder to complete than an income tax return; one man who filled it out maintains that the Peace Corps now knows more about him than either his mother or his wife.

Next, we ask candidates to take a comprehensive placement test. We learn about their language aptitude. We find out what they know about American and world history. We test their ability to think clearly and rationally. When all the examinations are scored, the Peace Corps has a "profile" of the applicant.

After we have received candid references from people who know the applicant, we invite promising candidates to a training program which lasts from ten to twelve weeks. Selection continues through training—and no candidate is ever sent overseas who has not completed a thorough training program.

During training, the applicant is given thorough medical and psychiatric exams. He is observed in classrooms and in field work. Meanwhile, our Civil Service Commission conducts for the Peace Corps a full investigation on each trainee. The examination is relatively costly—averaging about $350—but the revealed background information about the applicant, dating back to his school days, helps us to know just how suitable a candidate is for overseas service. As a result of this continuing assessment throughout training, for various medical, academic, or personality reasons about 15 percent of all trainees are dropped. But the process does not stop even there.

The final decision about a volunteer is made by a "Selection Board," which includes psychologists, psychiatrists, program officers who know the foreign country, and training officers who have watched the trainee work. It is our further policy to invite representatives from the host country—usually from the embassy in Washington—to participate as members of the selection panel. These members are not mere observers. They play a full role in evaluating all the information we have accumulated about each applicant. They can have a decisive voice in the selection of those who come to work in their countries as Peace Corps volunteers.

Out of the first twenty-five hundred to be sent overseas, we have had to bring just twenty-five back—and only ten of those could really be called "personal failures." The others were returned for compassionate or medical reasons.

There was yet a fourth question we asked ourselves: *Would our volunteers be able to work effectively overseas?* On this we could only wait for the record to speak. Perhaps by now it has done so.

Fifty-one volunteers were invited to Ghana. In one year they came into contact with some five thousand secondary school students. In Ghana this is almost 40 percent of all the students currently attending secondary schools. Volunteers also organized sports programs at many of the schools; one of them even coached his team to victory in the secondary school championship. Another volunteer developed a school farm to stimulate interest in vocational agriculture.

One hundred volunteers went to Colombia to work in rural villages. They are helping to build schools, aqueducts, bridges, roads, libraries, cooperatives, parks, and wells.

Last year in Nigeria, Peace Corps volunteers taught between eight and ten thousand secondary school students and almost five hundred college students. They organized science and art clubs, sports, and singing groups. One volunteer teaches a night course in American history and government for a class of about one hundred teachers, government workers, and other professional people.

In Tanganyika, our volunteers have full-time jobs running surveys and helping with on-the-job training of Tanganyikan fellow workers. They have also tutored students in engineering and mathematics, and one volunteer has helped to organize a youth club.

In Malaya our volunteers are serving as teachers, nurses, and surveyors. In Sierra Leone we are teaching in secondary schools. In St. Lucia we are teaching and working in health and agriculture programs. One of the teachers in St. Lucia has written back: "I consider that I have indirectly taught every 12-13 year old girl on the island through the weekly lesson guide I wrote in home economics."

These are just examples of what volunteers are doing in forty countries. But they are only part of the story. One of the fundamental reasons we have been able to come so far in so little time is the response we have received from every segment of American life.

Private industry has cooperated by granting employees leaves-of-absence to serve in the Peace Corps. International Business Machines, American Telephone and Telegraph, and General Motors are just three examples. The Caterpillar Tractor Company helped train our volunteers who went to Tunisia to serve as mechanics.

We have had tremendous support from labor unions. Organizations like the Communication Workers of America and the United Auto Workers are sponsoring leaves-of-absence for volunteers. American agriculture is helping also. The Farmers Union, the Grange, and the 4-H, for example, are administering programs for us overseas. So also are other private agencies like the YMCA and CARE, and organizations like the Near East Foundation and the Heifer Project.

The vast community of education has mobilized to help the Peace Corps. We have trained volunteers at forty universities—from Harvard in the East to the University of California at Berkeley in the West. Universities like UCLA are administering programs in partnership with the Peace Corps. Others like Ohio State are giving academic credit for service in the Peace Corps. Local boards of education who control public schools are giving leaves-of-absence to teachers who want to volunteer (New

York City, Chicago, Philadelphia, and Los Angeles are among them), and they have already approached us about hiring other volunteers when they come home from Peace Corps service. In a sense, therefore, the Peace Corps provides a genuine sabbatical for teachers and professors of very high quality indeed.

This great response to the Peace Corps by Americans from all areas of our population is one exciting reason why we believe the United States is benefiting as much from the Peace Corps as countries which receive volunteers, and perhaps more. But there is yet another reason why this is true—and it lies in the realm of what Peace Corps experience ultimately contributes to our country through the individual volunteers who go abroad. An African poet, Abioseh Nicol, has written:

"Go up-country, they said,
To see the real Africa. . . .

You will find your hidden heart,
Your mute ancestral spirit." [2]

Peace Corps volunteers have gone up-country to live and work, and they are seeing the real Africa and the real Asia and the real Latin America. They will return to the United States with the profound and enlightening experience of having lived among the people of foreign lands, not as "expatriates," but as persons who have eaten their food, lived in their houses, lived under their laws, spoken their languages, and shared their work. They will have a new understanding of the aspirations and the wants of the people with whom they share this turbulent globe —an understanding gleaned not from books or newspapers or hurried trips to capital cities, but the deep understanding which can only come from being a genuine part of the society one seeks to know. Each year five thousand of these Americans will come back into government services and private industry, continuing their work in foreign affairs, teaching, or simply enter-

[2] From "Up-Country," in *An African Treasury*, edited by Langston Hughes. © 1960 by Langston Hughes. Reprinted by permission of Crown Publishers, Inc.

ing the mainstream of American life. Wherever they go they will enrich the life of their communities. They will help create an America more profoundly aware of world problems and world responsibilities. They will bring back with them the second American revolution—a revolution of knowledge and increased capacity to work with other free men.

The Peace Corps movement in the United States, therefore, has taken on a significance far beyond the number of volunteers in service or the number of countries in which they work. For these numbers do not really explain the Peace Corps, the gratifying response of the American people to a demanding and difficult call to service, or the capacity of idealistic citizens to surmount the barriers of dozens of foreign cultures and languages and societies. For that answer we must look to the mainstream of the American tradition—the tradition summed up by Lincoln when he admonished his countrymen: "What constitutes the bulwark of your own liberty and independence? It is not our frowning battlements or bristling sea coasts. . . . Our defense is in the preservation of the spirit which prizes liberty as the heritage of all men, in all lands everywhere."

Let us admit that as fallible humans we have not always been true to this tradition. We have not always supported freedom abroad nor fully realized it at home. At times we have been aggressive in our attitude toward others or unjust in our attitude toward our own citizens. We have sometimes failed to understand the aspirations of people in other lands or to fulfill the hopes of our own people. Yet we believe that throughout our history we have retained an underlying dedication to certain principles. We would prefer to regard our lapses from these principles as temporary aberrations, mistakes, departures from what America should be, and do, and stand for. Today, behind the acts of diplomats, the words of politicians, the tortuous and hazardous conduct of the affairs of a powerful nation in times of danger, these principles are still deeply embedded in the lives of those who live across our land. And it is because the men and women of the Peace Corps inherit these beliefs, because they have absorbed them in the schoolrooms and churches, on the farms and in the cities of our country, that they have been able to cross barriers of language and culture, religious faith and social structure, to touch the deep chord of common hope and principle which belongs to all men.

The first of these principles is the conviction that the goals of the American revolution against colonial rule were universal goals. We were not simply fighting for American values; we were part of the greater revolution of man as he struggles to be free. Said Thomas Jefferson, "Every man and every body of men on earth possesses the right of self-government. They receive it with their being from the hand of nature." There are those who scorn such simple words as *freedom, self-government, the rights of man* as too simple and superficial for our complex, modern age. On the contrary, these words represent the basic revolutionary forces which are reshaping all continents. They also represent deep American convictions.

It is because our volunteers believe that no nation has the right to impose its will on others—that every individual should be free to follow the quest of his own mind and heart subject only to the loose restraints of a free society—that they welcome the opportunity to go out and help others carry forward this great work. We were in danger of losing our way among the television sets, the supermarkets and the material abundance of a rich society. Our debt of gratitude to the developing and emerging nations of the world is that they have reminded us of our own traditions, and given us a treasured opportunity to sacrifice and work once more for those principles which created our own nation. By letting us participate in their struggles they have given us a chance to find ourselves.

The second of these principles is our deep belief in a pluralistic world society. We built a country out of many lands and from people of a hundred different backgrounds and faiths. Today our President is the grandson of an immigrant to Boston. His predecessor came from the rural heartland of America. Our original states warred against each other for commerce and territory. And today there are still frictions and difficulties between regions and faiths and colors. But whatever success we have had in building a free nation stems from our confidence in a society which contains many societies. Our strength lies in the richness of our differences. And thus we do not fear the liberating discords of a pluralistic world society. We welcome what Gandhi called "the creative interdependence" of different lands, each free to follow and develop its own way of life, its own culture, and its own beliefs. We do not seek to impose a monolithic creed or system on the rich diversity of humanity. Thus our volunteers go out, not to change peoples, but to help them build their own societies as they themselves desire to build them.

The third of these principles is the belief in the power of individual moral conscience to remake the world—the belief so well expressed by men like Thoreau, that man has a higher duty than his obligation to party or state: a duty to conscience and common humanity. "Freedom is really in the mind," says Sierra Leone's poet Abioseh Nicol. In the last analysis it is not governments or organizations which will give fruition to man's hopes, but the energies and talents of millions of individuals working across national borders and dedicated to the service of mankind. Belief in man's inner moral conscience not only makes the welfare of the individual the first concern of man, but compels men to dedicate their energies to the service of others. "Let our affection flow out to our fellows; it would operate in a day the greatest of all revolutions." That, of course, is the root of the Peace Corps idea.

The last of these principles is man's optimism—the belief that all things are possible to men of determination and energy and a willingness to toil. This confidence came naturally to those who threw off the bonds of colonial rule and succeeded, with their own efforts, in subduing a wild and rich continent. But the same sense of man's limitless capacity is also moving now in Africa, in Asia, in Europe, and in Latin America. It has brought freedom to millions and inspires tireless efforts to build new societies.

These principles, of course, are not just American doctrines. They belong to all lands and to all people. They are fundamental human beliefs. On them rests the strength of nations. If from time to time any of us has momentarily lost sight of them, they have nonetheless remained at the moral heart of the universe. They have now stirred us to action in sending out thousands of Americans dedicated on a world scale to the same cause which built their nation. As this helps others to build their societies, it helps us to strengthen our own. And since these principles are equally basic to all, there is a profound implication in the swelling chorus of announcements that numerous other countries will begin Peace Corps efforts of their own. We welcome these efforts and stand ready to assist them.


# VOLUNTEER SERVICE

## REVIEW OF CONFERENCE DISCUSSIONS

The language of Mr. Shriver's review of United States Peace Corps efforts is in large measure matched by the successive conference contributions of numerous other delegates on the subject of this form of assistance. Touching on the experiences of various countries with the Peace Corps program, the plans of other developed nations along similar lines, and the recognition that purely domestic programs of the same type may also play an important role in internal development, the observations of the San Juan meeting confirm unmistakably the growing confidence in the institution of voluntary service as a recognized, useful, and effective instrument for the task of the developing nation. The concept of the volunteer, for work of the general Peace Corps type both at home and abroad, now seems assured of a permanent place in the vocabulary and plans of the economic development expert.

Tempering the enthusiastic, outspoken testimonials by various delegates to the United States Peace Corps programs operating within their respective countries, Vice-President Lyndon Johnson stresses the need for constant improvement through pooled experience. "We do not consider ourselves seasoned experts in this field," he says. "We may have some experiences which will be valuable, and whatever we do have we wish to share. But we are even more anxious to listen, and to learn, and to participate in the development of sound programs. We would like to find out whether others desire to expand services on a voluntary basis . . . [and] whether there are practical proposals for expanding local voluntary services."

### *What Makes the Peace Corps Work?*

Appraisals of the effectiveness of the Peace Corps, phrased in a variety of ways, reflect many observations in common but varied points of emphasis.

Conference Co-Chairman Emmanuel Pelaez, Vice President of the Philippines, feels that if indeed the Peace Corps is helping the American people rediscover themselves, it is also aiding its host countries to discover themselves for the first time. In his view, "The Peace Corps is successful because it is helping people with the heart. It is really the spirit of compassion that infuses the Peace Corps that makes it so welcome."

In his country's rural areas, declares El Salvador's Minister of Labor Alberto Ulloa Castro, the Peace Corps workers have "brought a spirit of generosity with them and have established a true friendship with the people." And in Sierra Leone, observes its delegate Banja Tejan-Sie, Speaker of the House of Representatives, the work of the Peace Corps has stimulated the mental, spiritual, and physical growth of the country.

For Tanganyika's Minister Amir Habib Jamal, the success of the Peace Corps in rendering volunteer service in an imaginative manner has been possible, "Firstly, because here was a country which did not have any historical ties with us organizing a program of voluntary service by waking up its people to its world responsibilities; and secondly, because in concept this volunteer service was moulded as a shirt-sleeve, down-to-earth kind of service where, to the individual, material gain was the least important factor."

The contagious quality of the idealism implicit in the Peace Corps idea is expressed by Ambassador Rishikesh Shaha, delegate of Nepal. "If the other developed countries of the world," he says, "join hands with the United States in widening the basis and scope of the Peace Corps concept, a healthy outlook for international cooperation will be created in the world. The countries like mine, which at the moment are merely on the receiving end, might share the impulse for this kind of voluntary service and come forward in due course to render such assistance as we can to other countries."

Looking into the past, when for many years Nepal had to depend upon religious missionaries, merchants, and traders as the chief agents for the dissemination of Western ideas and influences, Mr. Shaha recalls the fear which ultimately developed in the minds of his countrymen. Until the turn of the last century a popular local saying was "With the Bible comes the bayonet; with the merchant comes the musket." Becoming highly distrustful of outside influences, his people chose to live in isolation after the vast territory surrounding their country became a part of the British Empire. But he observes that the Peace Corps has not in any way become suspect. "It certainly is based on a noble and imaginative concept of humanitarian service, suited to the practical needs and demands of our time," he declares.

A very practical assessment comes from James Milton Weeks, Director General of Liberia's National Planning Agency. Announcing that the eighty-eight Peace Corps Volunteers who recently arrived in his country to teach in secondary schools will increase by 180 percent the number of college graduates teaching in Liberian secondary schools, he estimates that they will be able to affect directly about 90 percent of the total Liberian school population. He predicts that the Peace Corps teachers will decrease student dropout rates, improve basic curricula and indirectly have a great effect on the entire educational system. "The professional attitude of these new teachers," he declares, "should help materially in cutting down teacher absenteeism, late classes and improper preparation."

### Colombian Appraisal

The minutes of the San Juan Conference include a special message, sent from Madrid by Colombia's former President, Dr. Alberto Lleras Camargo, in which he says:

The anniversary of the Peace Corps is now being celebrated, and I wish to join my voice with the humble voices of millions of men and women throughout the world, in order to express admiration and gratitude for the collaboration being furnished in the development of the underdeveloped regions of the world by these volunteers serving a high ideal of international solidarity.

That cooperation cannot be measured, either in terms of money or material projects carried out under the leadership of the Peace Corps. What is of chief value in it is the spirit, the intent and the purpose. Citizens of the United States of America, for the most part young people who are barely out of the university, have accepted the responsibility of carrying to poverty-stricken or under-developed areas a higher material and moral ideal characteristic of societies that have had many opportunities to become organized and to achieve prosperity. They are not public officials. They do not act as political agents of a government. The remuneration they receive is insignificant, and they live anywhere under the same conditions as the nation which they have chosen as the theater for their friendly undertaking.

Having as the President of Colombia followed the Peace Corps experiment in my country, I feel boundless admiration for that idea and the way in which it is being carried out. Life in the villages of of the mountainous part of Colombia or on its plains is especially hard, even for those who have known no other type of existence. These young university men and women have accepted it with its privations and rigors. They have offered their simple and direct cooperation to improve the living conditions of this sector of human-ity, and to transmit the idea of joint effort and cooperation for pur-poses of more intensive use of their existing environment and re-sources—all this done basically with humility, sensitivity, and an eminently Christian spirit.

If the example of the Peace Corps were followed in each of our un-der-developed countries in the same way as some Colombian students have begun to follow it, there would be an incomparable instrument to transform materially the poverty-stricken and under-developed regions; but, above all, we would be using a tool effective enough to stop the forward thrust and fanaticism of the Communist enter-prises.

Only when it is discovered as the Peace Corps is discovering that the Western World is linked by ties, other than political convenience, which have their origin in the essence of their organization—only then will it be possible to succeed in the struggle against a revo-lutionary concept which has weakened very little in a hundred years, principally because of the incompetence of its adversaries.

The Peace Corps assistance program for Colombia was, in-cidentally, one of the very first. The agreement with the Colom-bian Government, signed in June, 1961, called upon the U.S. Peace Corps to select, train, and transport to Colombia a group of volunteers to work in community development, rendering help in a broad range of fields such as agriculture, rural education, low-cost housing construction, the planning and construction of rural roads and penetration roads into newly opened rural areas. For its part, the government of Colombia agreed to assign a Colombian counterpart to each of the communities where Peace Corps volunteers were to work, and to ensure that the host community had a genuine desire and interest in receiving Peace Corpsmen. By October of 1961 the specially trained volunteers, assigned in pairs, were distributed and began their work in twenty-eight towns and villages under the direction of a Colombian leader.

Although the original program called only for volunteers to serve in rural areas, more recently the Government of Colombia has also requested the assistance of social workers for assignment to low-income urban neighborhoods. Autumn of 1962 saw the first group of sixty-three of these in training in New York City, but with an interesting new feature. In order to establish coordination at the outset between the Peace Corps and their Colombian counterpart social workers, thirty community workers were selected in Colombia and were sent to New York City to be trained with the Peace Corps volunteers. As pointed out by Colombia's delegate, Minister of Labor Belisario Betancur Cuartas, this was done to avoid certain problems encountered in the earlier work, arising because the local volunteers in his country were not familiar with the preparation given the Peace Corps personnel, while the latter were not acquainted with the Colombian volunteers.

Commenting on the program as a whole, Mr. Betancur says, "If on balance we study carefully what the success of the Peace Corps program has been in our country we can conclude that it has been very successful, especially because the rural areas and rural communities have cooperated in a satisfactory manner and have demonstrated a positive attitude as a result of the inspiration and work of the U.S. Peace Corps and the Colombian volunteers." But continuing his frank appraisal, he notes the need in some cases for vocational training to raise the professional level of the Peace Corps volunteers in Colombia. "On the same basis," he says, "we consider that knowledge of Spanish on the part of the North American Volunteers is indispensable for the success of the program. We also believe that it is necessary to have better training in some of the specialties, and to focus on special abilities in order to obtain better results."

The Colombian delegate sees the Peace Corps largely in terms of hemispheric understanding. Says Mr. Betancur:

"We believe that the work of this international conference gives us a wonderful opportunity to study the future and the possibilities of this type of effort in the Latin American countries, and the impact that a program such as the Peace Corps might produce toward rapid and efficient solutions of some of our problems. We consider it very important that young North Americans inspired by ideas of service and understanding towards our country should come to our country, should meet and mingle with our people. Through exchange of experiences and knowledge there will come an effective social interchange. We believe this is important, especially as we recognize that these young volunteers will be future community and social leaders in the United States. As a result of their contact, and in contrast with previous generations in the United States, they will have clear ideas, better motives and better information on our own countries."

## The Volunteer vs. the Expert

Lest it be thought that these and the many similar responses to volunteer service presage a lesser role for the more traditional forms of assistance, a few nations hasten to point out that the need for the professionally skilled, salaried specialist remains undiminished. One of these is the United Kingdom, whose spokesman, Dennis Vosper, sees a place for each of the several alternative categories of manpower aid but reports that, in Britain's experience at least, the developing countries are continuing to ask for the expert. And, he says, "I very much doubt, from the structure of our society at home, whether we can meet the middle level manpower needs of any developing country entirely on a voluntary basis. I think there is a need for the experienced man as well."

But with the independence of so many formerly dependent areas Britain is finding it increasingly difficult to offer a permanent career overseas to talented young university graduates. It is no longer feasible to maintain a permanent manpower pool of skilled technicians with built-in-assurances of promotion. Thus, in the assistance to be rendered through salaried professionals Britain faces a major change from permanent overseas service to short-term service abroad as an incidental part of a home-based career.

"It is at present impossible to attract enough fully-trained people to meet all needs," says Mr. Vosper, "and the volunteer has proved well able to fill the gap which would otherwise have existed." Given quality and training, he feels, volunteers can make a real contribution. They can serve as auxiliaries, both as teachers and as technicians in the fields of industry and science. Moreover, he sees other advantages and desirable side effects of volunteer service. "It contributes much to the formation of character. . . . It sows the seeds of desire for further service overseas as part of a career."

New Zealand, too, is experiencing an increasing difficulty in recruiting experts for overseas service on anything other than a short-term basis. In discussing the field of volunteer service, which New Zealand has already begun, her External Aid representative Brien S. Lendrum stresses the importance of careful selection of volunteers to avoid romantic idealists or escapists, equal care in choosing their assignments, and a constant effort to maintain a "dialogue with the host country." In many cases New Zealand has found it highly productive to link the work of the volunteer with that of the expert, provided their duties are not identical so as to avoid possible resentments.

The British view that there is still a preference for the help of the experienced professional is supported by Herbert Owen Moran, Director General of Canada's External Aid Office. "My country does not force the paid advisor on any country," he says. "We act in response to the receiving country; the choice is theirs." But, he adds, "To date our experience has been that the countries have requested in the past—and are continuing to request today—the more highly skilled, the more highly qualified man. Many of the countries that we are aiding today have their own lower grades of middle level manpower and there is no purpose in our adding unemployment to that which already exists in those countries."

According to Dr. Walter Heller of the U.S., however, some figures on the United States Peace Corps show that it is possible to combine "volunteerism with experience." For example, about half the Peace Corps volunteers at work abroad are teachers, and half of these have had prior teaching experience. About 10 percent of all Peace Corpsmen hold master's or doctor's degrees. The degree of professionalism in the Peace Corps, he points out, may be judged from such facts as that one host country can count five doctorates in agronomy among its Peace Corps volunteers, another five medical doctors, and in one group there are ten seasoned commercial fishermen whose combined experience totals 298 years.

If there is any implication that the paid expert is more valuable to a developing country than the unpaid and perhaps less experienced volunteer, it is strongly challenged by Jamaica's Minister of Development and Welfare. Taking the widely accepted position that changes in popular attitude may often be no less important to a developing country than a supply of technical advice, Mr. Seaga recalls that his own people were willing to consider the concept of voluntary work themselves only after witnessing the activities of the United States Peace Corps in Jamaica. Before that, he says, Jamaican young people tended to insist on working at the level of the paid British expatriates.

"When the Peace Corps came to Jamaica," says Mr. Seaga, "they brought a breath of fresh air. They came and they mixed with the people. They worked closely with the people. And, because they did this, they have paved the way for our own people to understand that this [voluntary service] is a relationship which is acceptable; and, because it is acceptable, it paves the way for the government to organize them as a voluntary force which is capable now of providing a supplement to efforts such as the Peace Corps. . . ."

## VOLUNTEER PROGRAMS OF OTHER COUNTRIES

In terms of recent history the idea of using trained, qualified volunteers for service in the developing parts of the world seems to have arisen concurrently and independently in various economically advanced countries. Britain, Norway, Denmark, West Germany—these and others were all gaining experience and gathering data in this field when President Kennedy made his first, tentative proposals for a United States Peace Corps. On a limited scale, at least, and under various auspices, certain programs of this general type had been operating for a number of years.

But for the first time the disclosures of the 1962 San Juan Conference offer a measure of the stature and recognition which the whole institution of voluntary assistance has now achieved, with announcements by more than a dozen countries of plans to initiate or expand their own volunteer service activities. Some, like Denmark, Norway, and West Germany are preparing to move into the field of overseas volunteer assistance. Others, like Chile, Colombia, El Salvador, Honduras, and Jamaica are taking action to mobilize local volunteers from among their own people for programs of self-help, in the nature of domestic Peace Corps.

### New Zealand

Countries with volunteer programs already under way are broadening their scope. One of these is New Zealand, whose overseas aid spokesman Brien S. Lendrum reveals that his country's own small program of volunteer assistance, now three years old, will soon be expanded as a result of public enthusiasm generated by the United States Peace Corps activities. The New Zealand program is of the Peace Corps type but only partially financed by the government. In many other respects the two are similar.

### United Kingdom

Britain's volunteer program—nothwithstanding Mr. Vosper's emphasis on the paid expert—is in fact already one of the largest. While not yet on the scale of the U.S. Peace Corps, since 1958 it has provided some 600 volunteers to 50 countries for periods of a year or more, with at least 250 serving currently in 1962. Its entire administrative responsibility and the bulk of its financial support rests with private voluntary organizations—chiefly one known as Volunteer Service Overseas, whose funds are now being augmented increasingly by government grants.

The overseas work of the British V.S.O. is very similar to that of the U.S. Peace Corps. Teaching predominates, accounting for about 60 percent of its work. Many volunteers help in the regular schools as teaching assistants or teachers, but some serve in vocational training or trade schools. Other major fields to date include youth work, citizenship training, community development, agricultural improvement, technical services, and social work. The volunteers work both singly and in groups.

Most recently the United Kingdom has established a national coordinating body, the Volunteer Societies' Committee for Service Overseas, with representation of the various private volunteer organizations and the British Government. Its purpose is to promote, broaden and coordinate Britain's volunteer service abroad, while still leaving it in private hands. But additional government support is being provided, especially to increase the number of more highly skilled volunteers in the graduate category. About 60 of these are already at work in Africa and other areas, with 250 more scheduled to go overseas in 1963.

### Germany

A new volunteer program of the Federal Republic of Germany, already approved by the West German Parliament, is to be called "Learning and Helping Overseas." Under this scheme Germany will provide the help of young craftsmen, mechanics, and the like to developing countries. Inquiries are already coming in from young people wishing to volunteer, according to Federal Minister Hans von Merkatz.

It is planned that the activities of the West German volunteer program will be coordinated and supported jointly by the Bonn Government, German industry, and private organizations. Johan Wilhelm Funke of the Carl Duisberg Gesellschaft, a consortium of twenty-one German private agencies, advises that talks are being held with other Common Market countries on possible cooperative volunteer activities.

## Norway

"The concept of the Peace Corps has fired the imagination of the Norwegian people," says Admiral Rudolf K. Andresen, Secretary General of Norway's Agency for International Development. "In addition to assisting the economic and technical development of a country, it can also help in advancing general understanding. . . . We have reason to believe that amongst our own middle level manpower there is a desire, not to say a will, to participate in this Development Decade." The Government of Norway has called upon his agency to formulate plans by which the nation can best mobilize the enthusiastic desire, particularly among its younger generation, to assist in the developing countries. This will be done through a program of the Peace Corps type, on a modest scale at first but expanding as experience is gained. Norwegian Government Minister Mrs. Aase Bjerkholt foresees that teaching and vocational training are likely to predominate initially.

## Denmark

In Denmark a public subscription of funds for technical assistance projects has recently been completed and a portion of this is assigned to the Mellemfolkeligt Samvirke, a nonprofit, nongovernmental Danish organization for promotion of international cooperation. The money is being used to launch a small experimental program of volunteer assistance to developing countries.

Professor Mogens Pihl, a member of the executive board of the Danish Technical Cooperation Administration, describes the scheme in terms which indicate strong philosophical ties with the U.S. Peace Corps. The Danish volunteers are to be totally divorced from any religious or political ideology and will not be used as a weapon of the Cold War. Their duties overseas will be such as to permit them to operate in small groups and to share the living conditions of the local populace.

Candidates will be chosen with particular care by a committee, using psychological testing and observation during preliminary training. Personal qualities and character will be prime considerations. The projected minimum age of twenty will in fact permit a volunteer to undergo training and selection before reaching that age. In principle there will be no upper age limit and no rigid requirements as to education, provided only that the volunteer has the qualifications for his expected assignment.

Danish authorities currently favor a two-year period of service, including the time devoted to preliminary training. The training itself is to last four months, consisting of two months in Denmark and another two months upon arrival in the host country. The volunteers will serve without salary; but in addition to board and lodging they are to be given a small amount for pocket money and, upon completion of service, a small amount for re-establishment. After the first year of service, volunteers are to be entitled to three weeks of vacation with a small stipend for local traveling. As a special further condition they are expected to agree that, until six months after the end of their service, they will not write or make statements to Danish or foreign newspapers, radio and television stations without prior approval of their manuscripts.

## Japan

Mr. Zentaro Kosaka, Japanese Diet Member and former Foreign Minister, sees the principle of volunteer service as a possible partial solution to his country's problem of recruiting enough qualified, salaried experts to meet the overseas assistance demands. "Recognizing the increasing importance of the role being played by volunteers in the middle level manpower category," he says, "we are planning to institute a small-scale attempt along that line, with what we might call the 'junior expert.' " The plan, which Mr. Kosaka views as somewhat similar to that of the V.S.O. in Britain, is to send Japanese young people to developing countries in association with high level experts.

### Belgium

Belgium also is following the Peace Corps's activities "with the greatest of interest and is ready to make a positive contribution along these lines," says Maurice Brasseur, Belgian Minister of Foreign Trade and Technical Assistance. "Several private organizations in Belgium which are international in scope have for several years been undertaking voluntary aid programs benefiting the developing countries." One in particular is the Association of Voluntary Builders which, he points out, has also been cooperating with the U.S. Peace Corps volunteers.

Mr. Brasseur recommends a regular exchange of information among all the Peace Corps of the world. He further urges that other countries try Belgium's system of offering a year's exemption from military service for those willing to devote three years to assistance activities in a developing country. The inducement, he declares, has met with a very favorable response in his country.

### Voluntary Services at Home

Even beyond these growing efforts of the more developed nations, the San Juan discussions reveal that the emerging countries themselves are in many instances developing self-help programs, giving encouragement and assistance to their own private voluntary service groups, and otherwise promoting the concept of civic responsibility to contribute time and effort toward the national good. The idea of a domestic Peace Corps, of a systematic mobilization of volunteer skills, enthusiasm, and energy within a developing country, is becoming a reality in Latin America, in Asia, and in Africa.

In some areas the notion is not new. Vice-President Emmanuel Pelaez of the Philippines recalls the origins of two voluntary programs of the Peace Corps type operated by private groups in his own country.

One was begun in 1954, when Vietnam was partitioned and more than two million refugees from North Vietnam fled to the south. A group of young Filipinos, members of the Junior Chamber of Commerce, established "Operation Brotherhood," which sent doctors and nurses to help the victims of this mass migration. The program was well received and was later expanded to include agricultural and other technologists. Finally, it spread to neighboring Laos. A total of 388 volunteers were sent to Vietnam, where operations have since ceased, and 66 have gone to Laos to date. From the beginning there has been a counterpart training feature, and so far in Laos 373 local young people have been trained to take over the duties of the visiting Filipinos in such fields as medical aid and midwifery, electrical work, auto mechanics, carpentry, home economics, and rural development.

The second of these private voluntary efforts is the Philippine Rural Reconstruction Movement, now eight years old, which trains college graduates as multi-purpose rural workers to assist in community development projects in the Philippines. This operation today has workers in about 200 barrios, or communities. The goal of each Reconstruction Movement worker is to increase the income of every family in his assigned barrio by two hundred pesos a year. Experience has shown that in overcoming various problems—including civic inertia—it takes him about two years to make a success of his efforts. After that he is usually transferred to another nearby barrio, but continues to visit his old assignment once or twice a week for another two years. At the end of this time the village people themselves are generally able to undertake their own improvement projects without outside help. "They have learned," says the Philippine Vice-President. "They have been pulled out of the rut."

In a comparable way Niger's Minister of Education, Maidah Mamoudou, speaks of extensive local voluntary work in his own country. "Indeed," he says, "we have a Volunteer Corps, which for the present is concerned with highway work in joining villages, and such tasks as the construction of dams and schools—in other words, collective labor in these various fields."

Minister of Works Amir Habib Jamal of Tanganyika, where one of the earliest U.S. Peace Corps projects began, points out that voluntary service is by no means a new concept in his country. "Since our independence," he says, "the clarion call has gone to the country, to the people, to start self-help schemes. Our own system and concepts of local government are themselves based on the major premise of voluntary service." The response of the people has been tremendous, he reports. "A rugged mountain road completed yesterday; a water dam in progress today..."

But also, he continues, "A health clinic built with bare hands and the simplest crude techniques, waiting for the medical man to turn up. Or a simple school structure, lying empty without a teacher. This is the problem, the dilemma, the coming disillusionment." Lack of trained manpower—doctors, teachers, and others—threaten to make many of these self-help projects useless, he fears.

Some of the Puerto Rican efforts designed to enlist citizens to work for their own welfare and economic improvement involve what are called Mutual Assistance Programs, through which persons in their free time help each other construct their own homes. The Puerto Rican Government gives assistance to the extent of providing skilled supervision to enable the work to be done properly, and the necessary materials are furnished as loans which can be repaid on very reasonable terms. Apart from this scheme, Puerto Rican spokesman Frank Zorilla adds that there is a system of cooperatives and a program called "community education and organization of the community," through which the citizens of a neighborhood are encouraged to join their efforts in solving such community problems as the provision of a needed bridge or school building.

### Domestic Peace Corps

Appropriately choosing the occasion of the San Juan Conference for the purpose, Chilean delegate Hugo Galvez Gajardo has announced that his government is in the process of organizing a domestic program of volunteer service as a means of waging "an offensive war against poverty, disease, and ignorance." Mr. Galvez explains that the Chilean version of the Peace Corps was conceived after it became apparent that the activities of existing internal voluntary service organizations needed governmental coordination. The domestic Corps will work closely with the United States Peace Corps volunteers already at work in Chile.

Referring to the uncoordinated efforts of many types of volunteer workers in his country, Jamaican Minister Edward Seaga comments, "If we could channel their help and guide them, and ask them to give us their same service on a voluntary basis in those areas in which the government needs service more, we could create a force far greater than the sum of its parts."

"It is because of this," says Mr. Seaga, "that we in Jamaica have decided to organize our own Peace Corps. It will not be known by the name of the Peace Corps, for we have no war to fight. But it will be a national voluntary service, a national voluntary corps, it will be an 'operation brotherhood,' it will be something on the order of a gigantic voluntary organization which brings together the services of all those who are assisting in various ways to supply the intangible benefits of an added middle manpower force that no government can hire and that no government can measure."

As outlined by Mr. Seaga this force will be organized into various specialized units devoted to such fields as literacy training, community service, Community Chest fund raising, village athletic training, etc. It will contain units of doctors and nurses and professional people who will make their services available on a part-time basis, as a privileged group extending an arm of friendship to a less privileged people.

Meanwhile the Government of Honduras is taking immediate steps to create "a corps of peace volunteers on the internal level." With coordinated national planning, and using methods similar to those of the U.S. Peace Corps volunteers already working in Honduras, the domestic volunteers will help to carry out a program of community development financed in part with Alliance for Progress funds. Carlos Humberto Matute, Director of the Honduran National Economic Council, offers the hope that the Honduran effort may serve as a useful example to other nations and says, "We believe we have hit upon a new solution to our problems."

Summing up, United Nations Chef de Cabinet C. V. Narasimhan offers his own assessment of the voluntary service concept. The great merit of the Peace Corps, he observes, is that: "It takes advantage of the natural idealism and willingness-to-serve of people in many walks of life who have been eager to offer their services but who could not have been used by the normal technical assistance programs, bilateral as well as multilateral.

"Further, the Peace Corps supplements the human skills in the developing countries at a critical stage of development and at levels somewhat lower than those of the technical assistance experts.

"Last but not least, the most attractive feature of the Peace Corps is that they are not experts working as advisers, but idealists working with their hands as well as their hearts. . . ."

Stressing that there is room for all forms and channels of aid to meet the great needs of the developing countries, and that the Peace Corps has produced such remarkable results by evolving a kind of idealistic response, the United Nations representative says, "I would hope that other countries which have begun to experiment with this idea of recruiting Peace Corps men, junior experts, or whatever else they may be called, will have equal success."

Chapter

# VII

# International Cooperation for Development
# of Manpower Skills

## INITIAL RESULTS OF THE
## CONFERENCE

Certainly one of the most far-reaching consequences of the San Juan meeting was the enlistment of so many countries of the world in the spreading concept of more rapid diffusion of useful skills at the personal level through organized voluntary service. Conferences of this kind are normally expected to generate a wealth of valuable ideas and exchanges of useful information, as indeed this one did; but seldom does one yield so much immediate, positive, constructive action as was forthcoming in this field. The new or expanded volunteer programs announced successively by the numerous countries, and in some measure described in the preceding chapter, represent not mere conference resolutions but groups of very real people, doing or preparing to do at once a very real job where it needs to be done.

Not only in this comparatively new approach to development

aid, but also in the several more general avenues of skill development still inadequately explored in many countries, the
conference discovered a need for greater exchange of information and experience toward the mutual improvement of efforts,
and for a more telling attack upon the shared problem of middle level manpower for economic growth. To this end the assembled conference delegates took two concrete steps.

Endorsing the recommendation of their multi-nation Drafting Committee, the participating nations agreed upon the
immediate establishment of a small specialized secretariat, to be
set up in Washington, D.C., on a trial basis for a year, with the
specific functions of:

a. Winding up the work of the San Juan Conference, publishing
its technical papers and reports and making the conference results
available on a world-wide basis;

b. Providing for the international exchange of experience and
ideas on possibilities and problems of the increased use of volunteers
in the work of economic development, through either governmental
or private activities of the Peace Corps type by both advanced and
developing countries;

c. Diffusing information and experience on the role of private
enterprise, labor, and management in the training of nationals of
developing countries in middle level skills.

Although to simplify arrangements the United States Government agreed to supply a chief administrative officer and initial
staff and to meet the general operating expenses during the trial
year, provision was made for the interested governments and
the International Labor Organization to appoint liaison correspondents and to supply, at their own expense, such qualified
individuals as may be agreed upon for service in the secretariat's
work, and also for the work to be carried on in consultation and
cooperation with the various intergovernmental and private
voluntary organizations.

In presenting this resolution to the conference economist

Walt W. Rostow, Chairman of the U.S. State Department's Policy Planning Council, speaking to the final plenary session as Chairman of the Drafting Committee, noted that the device of a secretariat was the lightest administratively that the committee could propose. He outlined the several considerations that led to the proposal in this form:

"Essentially there were three questions we had to answer. First, why such a mechanism at all? The reason is that out of this conference—the thoughts which led into it, the decisions it has generated—there are certain very specific subjects on which our present knowledge is limited but on which there will be a wide interest in further information. And out of this came the notion of an experimental *ad hoc* clearing-house secretariat.

"Secondly, we had to ask ourselves, why not hand these functions to existing international organizations? For I can assure you my government, and clearly all of the governments represented here, are extraordinarily anxious not to proliferate international institutions where the functions overlap. The answer is very simple. It happens that in these narrow fields at this particular time there is no international organization engaged either in the work of collecting and unfolding information on the voluntary services, or on this even narrower but potentially interesting possibility of getting the private sector to enlarge its responsibility for training in the developing countries.

"Thirdly, why shouldn't the United States alone do it? Why do we provide for the presence in the secretariat not only of the ILO, but also of the other countries who may wish to contribute? Here again the answer is simple. For one thing, the United States doesn't command all the information, as we have seen during this conference in learning what other countries are doing; we may recall as an example Pakistan's information on the use of taxes and government administrative orders to move along training by the private sector. We just have an awful lot to learn and we need help in collecting that information and diffusing it. And finally, the interests involved here are not peculiarly American interests. Since we are all interested in this, provision in some way for sharing seems sensible.

"We are confident that these limited functions can be carried forward without any interference but rather by encouraging and strengthening the work of existing international organizations, and that the information generated by this secretariat or clearing house will be made available to interested governments and organizations on an effective basis. The conference has underlined how much we can contribute to each other, and we feel that the follow-up work of the secretariat should reflect this element of mutual concern and support."

The second action of the conference toward the same broad objective was to invite the International Labor Organization, and other international organizations concerned, to give high priority to the diffusion of information on accelerated training techniques designed to train persons rapidly in a wide range of needed manpower skills, particularly at the middle skill level. This includes applications of new technologies of training, outside the framework of formal education, to the immediate skill needs of the developing countries.

These are, of course, merely the first outward moves—the visible actions—of a congress of forty-three nations meeting for the common purpose of taking a new look at the problem of lagging development. The real achievements will be measured in future years when the consequences of these actions are evaluated in concrete terms, when the many lessons of the conference have been applied, and when the new programs guided by these lessons have borne fruit.

"What we have accomplished in these three days each delegation and government will, of course, judge for itself," said Dr. Rostow in presenting the Drafting Committee's summary report of the conference, "but permit me some personal observations."

"I recall the time when I worked in the secretariat of an international organization, the Economic Commission for Europe, in Geneva. We averaged there about three meetings a week. Incidentally, it was the narrowly defined working parties, rather than the high level committees or the commission itself, that usually hewed the wood and drew the water of international life. We got pretty hard-bitten about international meetings and used to judge them on two criteria. First, was some limited practical business carried a real, if modest, step forward? And second, did the exchanges lead to new general insights which might have a wider bearing on courses of action beyond the conference table?

"Judged by these two criteria I believe we have here some cause for satisfaction. We have been, I believe, good working partners. The conference has been the occasion for a dozen nations to press forward toward the creation or expansion of volunteer arrangements of the Peace Corps type. It has helped set in motion experimental bilateral arrangements and certain methods for quicker diffusion of middle level manpower skills, and stimulated the business community in the United States to undertake new efforts at home and abroad in the field of training nonemployee workers, which we hope will join with efforts going forward in other nations. All these initiatives represent specific germinal activities whose future none of us can predict. They may well prove to be steps on the way to more massive enterprises."

## THE WORK OF INTERNATIONAL AGENCIES

Many of the problems and solutions of main concern to the delegates at the International Conference on Middle Level Manpower lie exclusively within the province of national governments. Others are receiving attention on the basis of bilateral arrangements or by agencies within the United Nations system, such as the United Nations itself and the International Labor Organization, as well as other intergovernmental organizations such as the OECD.

It would be misleading to underemphasize the long-sustained efforts of these international agencies to date, and particularly those of the United Nations family, for indeed they furnish a background to the San Juan discussions and only serve to underline the magnitude of the world's common problem in manpower skill development. Some conference remarks of United Nations Chef de Cabinet C. V. Narasimhan touch upon this background generally, while at the same time drawing attention to one of the underlying reasons why the problem persists. Said Mr. Narasimhan in his final-day address:

"The International Labor Organization in the field of manpower studies and vocational training, UNESCO in the field of education and science, the Food and Agriculture Organization and the World Health Organization in their respective fields, the International Bank and its Economic Development Institute for the whole field of economic development, and the United Nations too with its schemes for fellowships, internships and training on the job—all these agencies and others not represented here have labored in this field for many years.

"Through the United Nations Special Fund we have been able to help the establishment of many training institutions in numerous countries, in various fields and at different levels of skill, and in doing so we have used the expertise and the knowledge accumulated over the years by our colleagues in the specialized agencies and the United Nations. In fact, practically half of the projects so far sanctioned by the Special Fund have been in the training field.

"But the international organizations have never had access to the kind of resources that could enable them to produce a really tremendous impact on this problem.

"I stress this point because it may easily be overlooked, when talking about the importance of investment in human capital, that such investment—sordid though it may be even to mention it—costs money. For example we can say now that in a developing country a polytechnic with a capacity to train, say, two hundred people a year will cost in fixed capital—in land, buildings, and equipment—about a million dollars, of which roughly half will be needed in the form of foreign exchange.

"So let us not overlook the need for financial capital even in the training of human beings and inculcation of human skills, because if we did we would be oversimplifying a somewhat complex problem."

For a closer look at the manpower development efforts of the various organizations in the United Nations family, much of this work is outlined by ILO's Director General David A. Morse in some excerpts from his conference address:

"The problems with which we have been dealing here are the very problems with which the ILO has been struggling very, very hard indeed in the last decades. As the international organization charged with primary responsibility in the field of manpower assessment, planning and training, the International Labor Organization has been designated as the focal point for coordination and action in this field by the United Nations and its specialized agencies.

"For some years now the ILO, working in cooperation with UNESCO, FAO and WHO, has been assisting countries in making accurate assessments of the manpower needed to implement development plans and of the resources available to meet these needs. . . . Approximately 75 percent of ILO's expenditure on field operations now goes toward the development of human resources, and an increasing percentage of this has been devoted to the middle level.

"The establishment of the UN Expanded Program of Technical Assistance and the UN Special Fund has given us a welcome opportunity to broaden our training activities and to set up national manpower planning machinery. The projects that ILO executes on behalf of the Special Fund, for example, aim principally at providing comprehensive training for industry—either modern industry or traditional small-scale industries capable of improvement and expansion. These are very large projects—as of this date totaling, as far as the ILO is concerned, some $72 million. They are backed by a whole complex of complementary projects essential to the proper organization of each country's manpower, such as the establishment of labor administrations, statistical and employment services, vocational guidance services and regulated apprenticeship systems for young persons.

"In recognition of the need for greater exchange of training information the ILO, in collaboration with several intergovernmental European organizations, has established an International Vocational Training Research and Documentation Center at Geneva. Plans are likewise well advanced for the setting up of an Inter-American Center of a similar character in Latin America.

"The other organizations of the United Nations family are equally concerned with the training of middle level manpower. For example, WHO last year devoted more than a third of its total number of projects to assisting member countries with such training. UNESCO is training primary and secondary school teachers. FAO has comparable programs in agriculture. The International Atomic Energy Agency has noted an acute shortage of trained laboratory personnel and electronics technicians in many developing countries, particularly in Africa, and this problem is foremost in the mind of this agency."

It is also of interest to note that the possibility of using volunteer technical personnel in their own work has been under study by the United Nations and its specialized agencies, and that in fact a set of principles applying to the use of such personnel has been agreed upon by the Economic and Social

Council and each of the agencies concerned. There have been discussions between these agencies and the United States Government on the possibility of using some American volunteers, and a number of projects have been tentatively selected as suitable for such assignments. On this prospect Mr. Morse makes the following additional observations:

"Since the manpower internationally available for assistance to other countries is at present limited, the association of such volunteer middle level manpower in some of our programs might greatly multiply the effectiveness of the assistance rendered, particularly by strengthening it at the working level. Moreover, there would undoubtedly be cases in which the availability of middle level volunteers would release nationals for training for which they could not otherwise be spared, and would thus also contribute importantly to the recipient countries' progress.

"The mission of the international organizations . . . is to encourage in the world the spirit of cooperation exemplified by the generous impulses of men who volunteer their energies and services to assist their fellow men in distant lands. A major result of this conference in Puerto Rico will be to give a new impetus to this common effort."

## TOWARD THE FUTURE

A long journey begins with one step. Is it in the right direction at last? Have we, as President Kennedy asks, really concentrated enough of our development effort heretofore on the aspect that counts most? Where do we go from here?

One of the great trends of our time is what economist Barbara Ward has called "the revolution of equality—equality of nations and equality of men." The fact of political equality is becoming more fully confirmed with each passing day as new nations achieve independent voices in world affairs and older nations break out of historical patterns of noninvolvement and enter into the councils of nations with new and vigorous interest. The achievement of economic equality is a matter of concern to all the nations of the free world.

The developing nations are fully aware of the long-run need to base solid programs of development upon a broad foundation of literacy and general education throughout all sectors of their citizenry. Nor are they any less anxious than in earlier years to preserve their own cultural heritage; but if we are to judge from the tone of the San Juan discussions, there is little today in the use of this familiar expression to suggest what was once often interpreted as mere resistance to innovation. So great is the pressure for economic growth, and so clear is the realization that this cannot come about without human skills, that to a large extent the immediate interest centers upon any and all avenues for emergency diffusion of vocational knowledge even if more general education must wait. And in this the new or enlarged programs of voluntary service disclosed during and since the conference will surely play a major part.

Of these, Dr. Walt Rostow calls our attention to the special significance, the possibly profound implications for the future, in the commitments of six of the developing countries to initiate domestic programs of this kind, operating within their own borders and carrying the communicative gift of volunteer assistance to their own heartlands. The importance of these decisions, he points out, arises from the fact that the ordinary process of development in its early stages tends to draw the educated and talented to the cities, to create a gap between the lives of those already drawn to the modern sector of society and those still caught up in the traditional ways.

"As one surveys the whole panorama of the developing nations in Asia, Africa, the Middle East, Latin America," Dr.

Rostow observes, "there is no one single requirement more urgent than that this gap be broken down. It must be broken down not only for the technical reasons we have discussed: the need to diffuse rapidly the essential skills required for modernization; it must be broken down as well for the most profound social and political reasons. If our common objective is to help create modern nations—independent, loyal still to their unique history and tradition, but capable of absorbing the fruits of modern science and technology—such nations cannot emerge merely by drawing to the vital and overcrowded cities the adventurous and talented.

"We have examined some technical economic reasons why rural and industrial development are fundamentally interdependent. But there are at least equally powerful political and social reasons why the young, the educated, and the privileged must go out and work with the poor and illiterate in their own country if modern, independent, free societies are to emerge from the development process.

"In developing nations it is not only the market for modern goods and services that must be enlarged, but the market place of ideas, of human communion, and a sense of common mission and destiny. Thus although they are by no means unique among the developing nations in acting to break down the urban-rural barrier, we have, I believe, special reason to congratulate Chile, Colombia, El Salvador, Honduras, Jamaica, and the Philippines for moving along the lines they have announced.

"Finally," Dr. Rostow comments, "the conference discloses a growing awareness that the possibilities of mutual help in the development process do not lie only between rich and poor nations. Being free, each of the developing nations is approaching its development in its own way, experimentally, in the light of its resources, its history, and its ambitions. As with each human being, the correct solution for the inevitable sequence of development problems for a nation must be a unique solution.

"Nevertheless, there is evident virtue in the intensive exchange of experience. In all conscience, we all have a great deal to learn about the development process. We must simultaneously learn and teach as we go, and as we go forward we will surely find enlarging opportunities with the developing nations to help one another in quite concrete ways; for, as the speakers of many countries have said here in different ways, the adventure of development is not merely for each nation, not merely for the more developed or the less developed nations; it is a great adventure for us all. Out of the struggle of nations to provide modern foundations for their independence and freedom we are learning the full measure of our interdependence, as nations and as men."

What then was achieved by the assembled statesmen at San Juan? Perhaps the best answer of all was given by one who spoke not as a statesman, not as a representative of any nation, but as an artist and champion of liberty who belongs to the whole world. The venerated cellist Pablo Casals, guest and observer at the closing session, told the conference:

"We have come from the tyranny of the enormous, awesome, discordant machines, back to the realization that the beginning and the end are man; that it is man who is important, not the mission; that it is man who accounts for growth, not just dollars or factories; and above all, that it is man who is the object of all our efforts."

# Epilogue

Events have moved swiftly since the close of the San Juan Conference. The new organization called for in the resolution passed by the forty-three participating nations, and now known as the International Peace Corps Secretariat, was created soon afterward with its headquarters in Washington, D.C., and Richard N. Goodwin, former U.S. Deputy Assistant Secretary of State for Inter-American Affairs, was named Secretary General. Through the months of 1963 to date the new secretariat has been engaged chiefly in helping numerous countries of the world to set up their own versions of volunteer service programs for work generally similar to that of the United States Peace Corps. Already at least five nations have done so, and the plans of several others are in various stages of completion.

Earlier this year the Netherlands Government established the Jongeren Vriwilligeres Korps (Youth Volunteer Corps), modeled very closely after the U.S. Peace Corps. Its first contingent of volunteers will be at work in Africa this autumn. There will be several hundred in the field by January, 1964, and the program is expected to build up to some three thousand volunteers within the first three years. In proportion to the Dutch population, by the way, this target is larger even than that of the U.S. program.

Denmark's originally modest scheme described in Chapter VI has recently been expanded with governmental support. Known as the Dansk Ungdons U-Landshjaelf (Danish Volunteer Service in Developing Countries), it is now proceeding with recruitment, selection, and training of volunteers on a larger scale. Its director, Mr. Jorgen Fenger, who not long ago visited the U.S. and several Caribbean areas to observe Peace Corps and similar operations, plans to have the first Danish volunteers working in three or four countries by late 1963 and about two hundred overseas within three years. In relation to Denmark's total population this too is comparable to the U.S. effort.

In April, 1963 Mr. Lasse Aasland was chosen as the first Director of Norway's new Fredskovps (Peace Corps), a private agency which has been given additional support through an allocation of government funds. The Norwegian Peace Corps expects to place its first twenty volunteers in English-speaking African countries by the time this book is published.

West Germany's President Dr. Heinrich Lübke formally inaugurated the German volunteer program Lernen und Helfen in Ubersee in mid-June, during President Kennedy's visit. The program is sponsored by the Deutscher Entwicklungsdienst, or German Development Association, a confederation of private voluntary agencies and various government departments, and the Bonn Government has budgeted the equivalent of U.S. $1.4 million for its first year of operation. The association plans to have 250 volunteers in service overseas by the end of 1964.

On the other side of the globe New Zealand is now enlarging its program following the recent establishment of Volunteer Service Abroad, Inc., patterned largely after the U.S. Peace Corps but operated as a private organization. Financed in part by public subscription and partly by a government grant, the organization is already recruiting its first volunteers for service this fall in Southeast Asian countries and the Pacific islands. Sir

Edmond Hilary, its president, plans to study U.S. Peace Corps operations in Washington this summer.

Among other developments of this kind, Italy's Foreign Minister has appointed a committee to study the possibility of an Italian Peace Corps to be known as Voluntari per la Pace, and the Argentine Government is pursuing its announced intention to send from two hundred to three hundred volunteer teachers to other Latin American republics. Argentina hopes to work through the Organization of American States in operating its "Teachers' Corps," for which some three hundred Argentine teachers had already volunteered by mid-1963. And Philippine Vice-President Emmanuel Pelaez has indicated that his country's planned domestic volunteer unit may later send Filipino volunteers to other Southeast Asian countries.

Meanwhile, as Chile, Colombia, El Salvador, Honduras and Jamaica move forward their announced plans for domestic volunteer units, discussions are being held on their possible association through the OAS in the creation of an "Alianza Corps" of hemispheric scope.

These are not the only nations contemplating volunteer assistance schemes. Others are conferring with the new secretariat, and 1963 may yet see the announcement of "peace corps" programs by several more countries whose plans are not quite ready for publication as this volume goes to press.

# APPENDIX

# 1

## INTERNATIONAL CONFERENCE ON

## MIDDLE LEVEL MANPOWER

### PARTICIPATING DELEGATIONS

**AUSTRALIA**

| | |
|---|---|
| David O. Hay | Australian High Commissioner to Canada |

**AUSTRIA**

| | |
|---|---|
| Erich Bielka-Karltreu | Secretary General, Foreign Office |
| Wolfgang Jungwirth | Development Assistance, Foreign Office |
| Wilhelm Schlag | Cultural Affairs, Consulate General, New York |

**BELGIUM**

| | |
|---|---|
| Maurice Brasseur | Minister of Foreign Commerce and Technical Assistance |
| Marcel Pochet | Director of Technical Services, Development Office |
| Pierre Deschamps | Counsellor of Cabinet for Technical Assistance Affairs |

**BOLIVIA**

| | |
|---|---|
| Guillermo Jauregui Guachalla | Minister of Public Health |
| Luis Sangines Uriarte | Executive Secretary, Ministry of Economy |
| Jaime Mendizabal Sanzetenea | National Planning Commission |
| Julio Mantilla Larrea | Office of Social Security |

**BRAZIL**

Flavio Amaro de Brito — Chief, Basic Industries Section, Servicio Nacional de Aprendizagem Industrial

**CANADA**

Herbert Owen Moran — Director General, External Aid Office

**CHILE**

Hugo Galvez Gajardo — Minister of Labor
Fernando Onfray — Solicitor

**COLOMBIA**

Belisario Betancur Cuartas — Minister of Labor
Rubin Dario Utria — Head, Regional Planning Section
Rudolf Martinez Tono — Director, National Vocational Education Center

**DENMARK**

Kjeld Philip — Minister of Economic Affairs
Mogens Pihl — Executive Board, Technical Cooperation Administration

**DOMINICAN REPUBLIC**

Nicholas Pichardo — First Vice President of the Council of State

Antonio Rosario — Secretary of Labor
José Selig Hernandez — Secretary of State for Agriculture
Pedro Mota Morillo — Assistant Director, National Employment Service

Rafael Felipe Sanabia Batista — Permanent Assistance Division, Agrarian Institute

**ECUADOR**

Armando Endara — Sub-Secretary, Ministry of Social Welfare

**EL SALVADOR**

Alberto Ulloa Castro — Minister of Labor
Fidel Gonzalez Angel — Chief, Ministry of International Affairs

**ETHIOPIA**

Bernahou Dinke — Ethiopian Ambassador to the U.S.A.

Richard R. Seppala — Finnish Ambassador to the U.S.A.
Wilhelm Breitenstein — Finnish Delegation to the United Nations

### FRANCE

Jean Basdevant — Director General, Office of Cultural and Technical Affairs
Luis Cappa — French Consul in San Juan, Puerto Rico

### FEDERAL REPUBLIC OF GERMANY

Hans Joachim von Merkatz — Minister for Bundesrat and Laender Affairs
Hans Guenter Kirschstein — Ministry for Economic Development
Werner Lamby — Regierungs Direktor, Ministry for Economic Cooperation
Hans Weiner — Personal Assistant to Minister von Merkatz
Dieter W. Holscher — Third Secretary of Embassy, Washington, D.C.

### HONDURAS

Carlos Humberto Matute — Director, National Economic Council
Marcial Solis — Dean of the Law School, University of Honduras

### INDIA

Surendra Kumar Dey — Minister for Community Development, Panchayati Raj and Cooperation
Sunil Dumar Roy — Indian Consul General in New York City

### ISRAEL

Mrs. Golda Meir — Foreign Minister
Ehud Avriel — Assistant Director General, Ministry of Foreign Affairs
Hanan Bar-on — Counsellor of Embassy in Washington, D.C.

### ITALY

Giuseppe Lupis — Under-Secretary, Foreign Ministry
Remo Paolini — Chief, International Organization Relations

152 : APPENDIX

| Angelo Altarelli | Director General of Placement, Ministry of Labor |
| Joseph Nitti | Secretary of Delegation |
| Carlo Logatto | Ministry of Public Education |
| Valentino Compagnone | Technical Expert in Manpower Training |

IVORY COAST

| Philippe Yace | President of the National Assembly |
| Mamadou Diakite | Assistant Chef de Cabinet |
| Jean Luc Toulouse | Cabinet Director |
| Honoré Polneau | First Councillor |
| Sylvette Gouclas | Secretary to Mr. Yace |

JAMAICA

| Edward Seaga | Minister of Development and Welfare |
| Warren G. Woodham | Director, Manpower Research Unit |

JAPAN

| Zentaro Kosaka | Member of Diet, former Foreign Minister |
| Kiyohiko Tsurumi | Counsellor, Economic Cooperation Bureau, Foreign Office |
| Nobura Takeshita | Member of Diet |
| Soichiro Itoh | Member of Diet |
| Yoshitake Sasaki | Member of Diet |
| Isaburo Mukumoto | Japanese Embassy, Washington, D.C. |

LIBERIA

| James Milton Weeks | Director General, National Planning Agency |

MALAYA

| Ong Yoke Lin | Malayan Ambassador to the U.S.A. |
| K. Pathmanaban | Assistant Secretary, Ministry of Labor |
| K. Y. Chen | Personal Assistant to the Ambassador |

NEPAL

| Rishikesh Shaha | Special Ambassador, with rank of Minister |
| Miss Bhinda Malla | Second Secretary of Embassy, Washington, D.C. |

NETHERLANDS

| Jan Meijer | Chairman, Interdepartmental Committee for Technical Assistance |

W. C. J. van Leeuwen — Acting Chief of General Affairs, Netherlands Antilles

### NEW ZEALAND
Brien S. Lendrum — Deputy Head, External Aid Division, Ministry of External Affairs

### NIGER
Maidah Mamoudou — Minister of Education

### NIGERIA
Joseph Modupe Johnson — Minister of Labor
Miss Mary A. Ekpiken — Occupational Research and Classification, Labor Office
A. O. Kayode — Private Secretary to Minister Johnson

### NORWAY
Mrs. Aase Bjerkholt — Minister for Family and Consumer Affairs
Johan Galtung — Sociologist
Kalmar Oksnes — Chairman, Committee on Norwegian Peace Corps
Admiral Rudolf K. Andresen — Secretary General, Agency for International Development
Arne Arnesen — Foreign Office

### PAKISTAN
Zahiruddin Ahmed — Joint Secretary, Finance Ministry

### PHILIPPINES
Emmanuel Neri Pelaez — Vice President
Amelito R. Mutuc — Philippine Ambassador to the U.S.A.
Vicente R. Jayme — Deputy Director, Program Implementation Agency and Vice President, Philippine National Bank
José V. A. Cruz — Technical Assistant to the Vice President
Major Angelo S. Cruz — Aide de Camp to the Vice President
D. Neri — Technical Advisor to the Vice President
Mrs. R. Neri — Private Secretary to the Vice President
Mrs. P. Chiongbian — Technical Advisor

### ST. LUCIA
G. F. L. Charles — Chief Minister

### SIERRA LEONE

| | |
|---|---|
| Banja Tejan-Sie | Speaker of the House of Representatives |
| Ahmad D. Wurie | Minister of Education |
| C. Stevens | Member of the Opposition |

### SWEDEN

| | |
|---|---|
| Mrs. Ulla Lindstrom | Minister Without Portfolio to the United Nations |
| Arne Bjornberg | Secretary General, Board for International Aid |
| Bertil Bolin | Trade Union Federation |

### SWITZERLAND (Observer)

| | |
|---|---|
| Lukas Burckhardt | Labor Attaché, Swiss Embassy, Washington, D.C. |

### TANGANYIKA

| | |
|---|---|
| Amir Habib Jamal | Minister of Communications, Power and Works |

### THAILAND

| | |
|---|---|
| Pin Malakul | Minister of Education |
| Nai Boonchana Atthakor | Director General, Thai Technical and Economic Corporation |
| Sakda Saibua | Chief, Research and Project Division, T.T.E.C. |
| Nob Palakawongsa | Director, External Relations Division, Ministry of Education |

### TUNISIA

| | |
|---|---|
| Mondher Ben Ammar | Secretary of State for Public Health and Social Affairs |
| Habib Bourguiba, Jr. | Tunisian Ambassador to the U.S.A. |
| Mohammed Ennaceur | Chef de Cabinet |
| Miss Jaouida Ghileb | Chef de Service, Secretariat for Planning and Finance |

### UNITED KINGDOM

| | |
|---|---|
| Dennis F. Vosper | Secretary for Technical Cooperation |
| William J. Smith | Head, Social Development Department, Department of Technical Cooperation |
| H. F. Brien Fane | Labor Counsellor, U.K. Embassy, Washington, D.C. |

## UNITED STATES

| | |
|---|---|
| Lyndon B. Johnson | Vice President |
| W. Willard Wirtz | Secretary of Labor |
| Anthony J. Celebrezze | Secretary of Health, Education and Welfare |
| Robert Sargent Shriver, Jr. | Director, Peace Corps |
| Walter Heller | Chairman, President's Council of Economic Advisors |
| Walt W. Rostow | Chairman, Policy Planning Council, Department of State |
| James M. Quigley | Assistant Secretary of Health, Education and Welfare |
| George L. P. Weaver | Assistant Secretary of Labor |
| Frank M. Coffin | Deputy Administrator, A.I.D. |
| Teodoro Moscoso | Coordinator, Alliance for Progress |
| Richard M. Goodwin | Deputy Assistant Secretary of State for Inter-American Affairs |

## VENEZUELA

| | |
|---|---|
| Oscar Palacios Herrera | President, Institute of Educative Cooperation |
| Elias D. Lopez Ortega | Director, Institute of Educative Cooperation |
| Godofredo Gonzales | Minister of Development |
| Juan J. Paez Maya | Director of Handicraft, Industrial and Commercial Education, Ministry of Education |
| Raul Valery Salvatierra | Director of Social Welfare, Ministry of Labor |
| Aquiles Torrealba | Chief, Manpower Division, Ministry of Labor |
| Espiritu Santos Mendoza | Director of Special Affairs, Ministry of Health |

## ASIAN PRODUCTIVITY ORGANIZATION (APO)

| | |
|---|---|
| Ichiro Oshikawa | Secretary General |
| Lie Kwen-Hi | Assistant Program Officer |

## FOOD AND AGRICULTURE ORGANIZATION (FAO)

| | |
|---|---|
| Harold Vogel | Director, North American Region |

### INTERNATIONAL BANK FOR RECONSTRUCTION AND DEVELOPMENT (WORLD BANK)

| | |
|---|---|
| Michael Hoffman | Director, Development Advisory Service |

### INTER-GOVERNMENTAL COMMITTEE ON EUROPEAN MIGRATION (ICEM)

| | |
|---|---|
| Bastiaan W. Haveman | Director |
| Ernest Rahardt | |
| Jacinto Maselli | |

### INTERNATIONAL LABOR ORGANIZATION (ILO)

| | |
|---|---|
| David A. Morse | Director General |
| R. M. Lyman | Chief, Manpower Division |

### ORGANIZATION FOR ECONOMIC COOPERATION AND DEVELOPMENT (OECD)

| | |
|---|---|
| Charles W. Adair | Deputy Secretary General |
| Munir Benjenk | Assistant Director for Cooperation, Development Department |

### UNITED NATIONS

| | |
|---|---|
| C. V. Narasimhan | Chef de Cabinet |
| James Keen | Chief, Fellowship Training Board |
| Edmond Janssens | Caribbean Regional Representative, Technical Assistance Board |

### UNITED NATIONS EDUCATIONAL, SCIENTIFIC AND CULTURAL ORGANIZATION (UNESCO)

| | |
|---|---|
| Arthur Gagliotti | Director, New York Office |

### WORLD HEALTH ORGANIZATION (WHO)

| | |
|---|---|
| John C. Cutler | Deputy Director, Pan American Sanitary Bureau |

### AMERICAN COUNCIL ON EDUCATION

| | |
|---|---|
| Lawrence E. Dennis | Executive Associate |

### AMERICAN COUNCIL OF VOLUNTARY AGENCIES FOR FOREIGN SERVICE

| | |
|---|---|
| Charlotte E. Owen | Executive Director |
| Paul Bernick | Secretary, Board of Directors |

CARL DUISBERG GESELLSCHAFT

| | |
|---|---|
| Johan Wilhelm **Funke** | Secretary, Gespraechskreis Entwicklungshelfer |

ENGLISH VOLUNTARY SOCIETIES' COMMITTEE FOR SERVICE OVERSEAS

| | |
|---|---|
| Duncan Mackintosh | Executive Chairman |

INSTITUTE OF INTERNATIONAL EDUCATION

| | |
|---|---|
| Alfred Sims | Vice President for Operations |

OPERATION BROTHERHOOD

| | |
|---|---|
| Oscar Arellano | Chairman |

ORGANIZATION FOR REHABILITATION AND TRAINING (ORT)

| | |
|---|---|
| Max Braude | Director General |

*Advisers to the United States (Host) Delegation*

| | |
|---|---|
| Karl F. Bode | Chief, Planning Assistance Division, Research, Evaluation and Planning Assistance Staff, Agency for International Development |
| Francis P. Carter | Deputy Inspector General, Foreign Assistance, Department of State |
| Charles C. Diggs | House of Representatives |
| Edwin R. Durno | House of Representatives |
| Rashi Fein | U.S. Council of Economic Advisors |
| Abe Fortas | Adviser to the Vice President |
| Bartlett Harvey | Chief, Economic Programs Division, Program Coordination Staff, Agency for International Development |
| Walter Kotchnig | Director, Office of International, Economic and Social Affairs |
| John Leslie | Director, Office of Information, Publications and Reports, Department of Labor |
| Howard Rosen | Office of Manpower, Automation and Training, Department of Labor |
| Edward C. Sylvester | Assistant to the Assistant Secretary of International Affairs, Department of Labor |
| Thomas Watson | Chairman, Board of Directors, International Business Machines Co. |

158 : APPENDIX

| | |
|---|---|
| Seymour Wolfbein | Director, Office of Manpower, Automation and Training, Department of Labor |
| Adam Yarmolinsky | Special Assistant to the Secretary of Defense |
| Prof. A. J. Jaffe | Director, Manpower and Population Program, Bureau of Applied Social Research, Columbia University |

# APPENDIX

# 2

## INTERNATIONAL CONFERENCE ON

## MIDDLE LEVEL MANPOWER

### TECHNICAL AND SUMMARY PUBLICATIONS

Brunner, Ken August (U.S. Dept. of Health, Education and Welfare), *The Training of Sub-Professional Personnel in the United States*, Technical Paper No. 20.

Conference Secretariat, *Daily Summary of Proceedings*, separate issues of October 10, 11, and 12, 1962.

Eason, John C. (U.S. Dept. of Health, Education and Welfare), *Health Manpower Resources for Twenty-three Selected Countries*, Technical Paper No. 19.

Ennaceru, Mohammed (Government of Tunisia), *Elements of a Manpower Program for Developing Countries: The Tunisian Experience*, Technical Paper No. 33.

Fein, Rashi (U.S. Council of Economic Advisors), *Integration of Educational Planning with Economic and Social Planning*, Technical Paper No. 9.

Fisher, Paul (U.S. Agency for International Development), *The Role of Middle Level Manpower in Social and Economic Development*, Technical Paper No. 6.

Food and Agriculture Organization, *Middle Level Manpower in Agriculture*, Technical Paper No. 11.

Galtung, Johan (Institute for Social Research, Oslo, Norway), *Notes on the Sociology of Middle Level Manpower Assistance*, Technical Paper No. 34.

160 : APPENDIX

Goldstein, Harold (U.S. Dept. of Labor), *Occupational Composition Patterns in Various Economies at Different Levels of Development*, Technical Paper No. 16.

Government of Denmark, *The Administration of Volunteer Service Programs*, Technical Paper No. 22.

Government of France, *La France et la Formation des Cadres des Pays en Voie de Developpement*, Technical Paper No. 32.f.

Government of India, *Elements of a Manpower Program for Developing Countries: The Indian Experience*, Technical Paper No. 5.

Government of Israel, *Manpower Planning and Training of Middle Level Personnel in the Technical Field*, Technical Paper No. 14.

Government of the Netherlands, *The Netherlands Associate Expert Scheme*, Technical Paper No. 26.

Government of Thailand, *Manpower Development in Undeveloped Countries*, Technical Paper No. 31.

Government of the United Kingdom, *The Future of Technical Assistance: The Place and Contribution of the Volunteer*, Technical Paper No. 25.

Harary, Joseph A. (Conference Secretariat), *Manpower Training by Private American Companies Abroad*, Technical Paper No. 21.

Hoffman, Michael L. (International Bank for Reconstruction and Development), *Middle Level Manpower in Developing Economies*, Technical Paper No. 13.

Inter-Governmental Committee for European Migration, *The Impact of Qualified Immigrants on Developing Areas*, Technical Paper No. 27.

———, *Vocational, Professional and Leadership Training*, Technical Paper No. 28.

———, *Language Training for Immigrants to Developing Countries*, Technical Paper No. 29.

———, *Economic Development through Migration*, Technical Paper No. 30.

Iverson, R. W. (U.S. Peace Corps), *Peace Corps Training: Lessons of the First Year*, Technical Paper No. 24.

Kelley, E. Lowell (U.S. Peace Corps), *The Selection of Peace Corps Volunteers*, Technical Paper No. 23.

McCauley, John S. (U.S. Dept. of Labor), *Employer Responsibility for Developing Middle Level Manpower*, Technical Paper No. 17.

Oshikawa, Ichiro, *The Asian Productivity Organization*, Technical Paper No. 36.

Peace Corps, *Medical Mid-Level Sub-Professional Training*, Technical Paper No. 2.

———, *Trades Training Center Plan*, Booklet.

———, *Training Center Plan for Building Construction Occupations (Village and Community Development)*, Booklet.

———, *TYPE Engineer Training Center*, Booklet.

Rostow, Walt W., et. al. (MLM Conference Drafting Committee), *Summary Report of the Conference*, Document No. 20.

Shapiro, T. R., Adams, W. and Gordon, J. (Bureau of Applied Social Research, Columbia University, New York), *Labor Supply and Demand for Middle Level Occupations in Developing Countries*, Technical Paper No. 8.

Sobel, Irvin (Washington University, St. Louis), *The Relationship between Education and Productivity*, Technical Paper No. 4

Tachi, Minoru (Institute of Population Problems, Japan), *Forecasting Manpower Resources: Population and Labor Force*, Technical Paper No. 35.

Woodham, Warren (Government of Jamaica), *The Elements of a Manpower Program for Developing Countries: A Jamaican Case*, Technical Paper No. 7.

World Health Organization, *Recent and Current Activities of the World Health Organization Relating to Middle Level Manpower*, Technical Paper No. 12.

Zack, Arnold M. (Conference Secretariat), *Trade Unions and the Development of Middle Level Manpower*, Technical Paper No. 3.

APPENDIX

# 3

SUPPLEMENTARY BIBLIOGRAPHY ON
MIDDLE LEVEL MANPOWER, VOLUN-
TARY SERVICE PROGRAMS, AND
SOCIAL AND ECONOMIC DEVELOP-
MENT

The selected readings listed here under these three general headings do
not in any sense comprise an exhaustive bibliography. In social and economic development, particularly, the literature is so vast that it is patently
impractical to include here more than a limited number of selections
bearing upon the specific topics discussed in the sessions of the San Juan
International Conference on Middle Level Manpower.

The present bibliography was especially prepared for the conference
secretariat through the assistance of the Legislative Reference Service of
the United States Library of Congress. Each entry is given under the principal heading to which it appears to be most usefully relevant, but in many
cases may relate also to one or both of the other headings. Some of the
listed publications bear titles which may seem remote from the general
topic heading, but are included because they contain material adjudged to
be pertinent.

Bearing in mind that the term *middle level manpower* is not precise and
is only now coming into general use, later bibliographies on this subject
will undoubtedly contain many more entries which should rightfully be
included here. The present selections under this heading have been made
with special consideration to the international aspects of middle level

manpower development, and particularly to its development in the emerging economies of Asia, Africa, and the Western Hemisphere.

## I. MIDDLE LEVEL MANPOWER

### 1. Bibliographies

International Labour Office, Library. *Bibliography on Labour Law.* Geneva, 1958, 104 p. (Bibliographic Contributions No. 13).
————, *Bibliography on Vocational Training.* Geneva, 1957. 39 p. (Bibliographic Contributions No. 12).
————, *Bibliography on Workers' Education.* Geneva, 1956. 41 p. (Bibliographic Contributions No. 11).
Patai, Raphael. *Jordan, Lebanon and Syria: An Annotated Bibliography.* New Haven, Connecticut, Human Relations Area Files, 1957. 289 p.
Shostak, Arthur B. *Management and Labor Problems in Economic Development: Selected References.* Princeton, New Jersey, Princeton University, Industrial Relations Section, November, 1959. (No. 90).
Simpson, Keith, and Hazel C. Benjamin. *Manpower Problems in Economic Development: A Selected Bibliography.* Princeton, New Jersey, Princeton University, Industrial Relations Section, 1958. 93 p.
Sufrin, Sidney C., and Frank Eugene Wagner. *A Brief Annotated Bibliography on Labor in Emerging Societies.* Syracuse, New York, Syracuse University, Center for Overseas Operations, 1961. 64 p.
Talbot, P. *A Selected Bibliography: Asia, Africa, Eastern Europe, Latin America.* New York, American Universities Field Staff, Inc., 1960. 533 p.
Vermilya, Adeline T. *Manpower Surveys and Education Projections in Economic Development: Selected References.* Princeton, New Jersey, Princeton University, Industrial Relations Section, May, 1961. (No. 99).

### 2. Books and Pamphlets

Allbee, Lewis. *Education as an Implement of U.S. Foreign Policy* (1938-1948). Ann Arbor, Michigan, Edwards Brothers, Inc., 1948. 270 p.
American Management Association, Research and Development Division. *The Management of Scientific Manpower;* with a Special Supplement on Engineering Education. New York, 1953. 160 p.
Angel, Juvenal Londono. *Careers in the Field of Export, Import and Foreign Operations.* New York, World Trade Academy Press, 1961. 26 p.

*An Important Answer to Present World Needs.* Waverly, Iowa, Self Help, Inc. (not dated) 3 p.

*The Apprentice Experts.* New York, The Ford Foundation, February, 1960. 49 p.

Aronson, Robert L. and John P. Windmuller, editors. *Labor, Management, and Economic Growth: Proceedings of a Conference on Human Resources and Labor Relations in Underdeveloped Countries.* Ithaca, New York, Institute of International Industrial and Labor Relations, Cornell University, March, 1954. 251 p.

Barker, Sir Ernest. *National Character and the Factors in Its Formation.* London, Methuen and Co., Ltd., 1948. 268 p.

Billerbeck, Klaus. *Mobilization of Manpower Potential in Asia and Africa.* Translation: Jean Bollkamper. Hamburg, Hamburg Archives of World Economy, 1961. 169 p.

Blood, Jerome W., editor. *Optimum Use of Engineering Talent: Meeting the Need for Technical Personnel.* New York, American Management Association, 1961. 416 p.

Bodenman, Paul S. *American Cooperation with Higher Education Abroad.* U.S. Department of Health, Education and Welfare, Office of Education, Bulletin 1957, No. 8. Washington, U.S. Government Printing Office, 1957. 211 p.

Caribbean Commission. *Development of Vocational Education in the Caribbean.* Port-of-Spain, Trinidad. Caribbean Commission, 1953.

CIRF. *International Vocational Training Information and Research Centre.* Geneva, International Labour Office, 1961. 4 p.

Cleveland, Harlan, and Gerard J. Mangone. *The Art of Overseasmanship.* Syracuse, New York, Syracuse University Press, 1957. 150 p.

Cleveland, Harlan, Gerard J. Mangone, and John Clarke Adams. *The Overseas Americans.* New York, McGraw-Hill Book Co., Inc., 1960. 316 p.

*The Colombo Plan Story.* Colombo, Colombo Plan Bureau, 1961. 44 p.

Ellsworth, Maryann D. *Problems of Education and of Vocational, Scientific and Technical Training in Countries in Process of Development.* Washington, The Library of Congress, Legislative Reference Service, 1961. Processed. 41 p.

Food and Agriculture Organization of the United Nations. *Training Rural Leaders.* Shantan Bailie School, Kamsu Province, China. Washington, 1949. 136 p.

*The Ford Foundation and Foundation Supported Activities in India.* New York, The Ford Foundation, 1955. 106 p.

*The Ford Foundation and Pakistan.* New York, The Ford Foundation, 1959. 44 p.

*The Ford Foundation Program in Burma 1953-1958.* New York, The Ford Foundation, January, 1959. 16 p.

Foreign Policy Association-World Affairs Center. *Careers in World Affairs: at Home and Abroad.* Garden City, New York, Doubleday and Co., 1961. 140 p.

Galenson, Walter, editor. *Labor and Economic Development.* New York, John Wiley and Sons, Inc., 1959. 304 p.

Ghana, Establishments Office. *Manpower Survey of Ghana.* Prepared by The Ford Foundation, Edward Hollander, Consultant, Accra, 1960. Variously paged. Mimeographed.

Ginsberg, Eli. *Human Resources: the Wealth of a Nation.* New York, Simon and Schuster, 1958. 183 p.

Greenough, Richard. *Africa Calls; Development of Education, the Needs and Problems.* Paris, UNESCO, 1961. 50 p.

Griffith, Alison, editor. *The Role of American Higher Education in Relation to Developing Areas.* Washington, The American Council on Education, 1961. 70 p.

Harbison, Frederick H. *The Comparative Study of High-level Manpower in Developing Societies, a Tentative Framework.* Princeton, New Jersey, Inter-University Study of Labor Problems in Economic Development, 1961. 20 p. Mimeographed.

Harbison, Frederick H. "Human Resources Development Planning in Modernizing Economics." Geneva, *International Labour Review,* v. 85, May, 1962. p. 435-458.

Harbison, Frederick, and Abdelkader Ibrahim. *Human Resources for Egyptian Enterprise.* New York, McGraw-Hill Book Co., Inc., 1958. 230 p.

High, Sidney C., Jr. *Vocational Industrial Education in Newly Developing Countries. A Case Study of the Philippines, 1951-1956.* Stanford, California, Stanford University, 1960. 68 p. (Stanford University's School of Education, Comparative Education Series, Study No. 1.)

Hoffman, Paul G. *The Greatest Challenge of All.* New York, Public Affairs Committee, Inc., 1961. 12 p. (Public Affairs Pamphlet No. 313.)

———, *One Hundred Countries: One and One Quarter Billion People.* Washington, Albert D. and Mary Lasker Foundation, 1960. 62 p. V. The Key Importance of Adequate Preinvestment Operations, p. 34-43.

Institute of International Education. *A Report to the President of the United States.* New York, Institute of International Education, 1961. 15 p.

———, *Committee on Educational Interchange Policy.* New York, Institute of International Education, 1961. 25 p. Bibliography p. 22-25.

Inter-African Labour Institute. *The Human Factors of Productivity in Africa.* London, The Institute, 1956. 158 p.

International African Institute. *Social Implications of Industrialization and Urbanization in Africa South of the Sahara.* Prepared under the auspices of UNESCO. Paris, UNESCO, 1956. 743 p.

International Cooperation Administration. *Technical Cooperation in Education.* Department of State Publication 7024. Washington, U.S. Government Printing Office, 1960. 31 p.

International Labour Conference, Forty-sixth Session, Geneva, 1962. *Fourth Item on the Agenda: Vocational Training. Report IV-(2).* Geneva, International Labour Office, 1962. 101 p.

International Labour Office. *Bibliography of Industrial Relations.* Geneva, International Labour Office, 1955. 103 p.

International Labour Office. *International Standard Classification of Occupations.* Geneva, 1958. 236 p.

International Labour Office. *Labour Survey of North Africa.* Geneva, 1960. 473 p. (New Series, No. 60)

————, *Report to the Government of Ghana on the Development of an Employment Information Programme.* Geneva, 1959. 26 p.

————, *Report to the Government of Ghana on the Establishment of a National Apprenticeship System.* Geneva, 1961. 54 p.

————, *Report to the Government of the Sudan on the Development of Cooperatives.* Geneva, 1960. 53 p.

————, *Report to the Government of Thailand on a Productivity Demonstration Mission* (September-November 1958). Geneva, 1959. 19 p.

————, *Report to the Government of Thailand on Handicrafts Training in the Chachoengsao Pilot Project.* Geneva, 1960. 33 p.

————, *Report to the Government of Thailand on the Training of Supervisors.* Geneva, 1959. 19 p.

————, *Report to the Government of Trinidad and Tobago on the Establishment of a Manpower Information Programme.* Geneva, 1960. 32 p.

————, *Report to the Government of Turkey on Technical and Vocational Education.* Geneva, 1959. 70 p.

Iran, Ministry of Labor. *National Manpower Resources and Requirements Survey.* Iran, 1958. Washington, Governmental Affairs Institute, 1959. 90 p.

Jaffe, Abram J. and Charles D. Stewart. *Manpower Resources and Utilization.* New York, John Wiley and Sons, 1951. 532 p.

Maunder, W. *Employment in an Underdeveloped Area; a Sample Survey of Kingston, Jamaica.* New Haven, Connecticut, Yale University Press, 1960. 215 p.

Metraux, Guy S. *Exchange of Persons: The Evolution of Cross-Cultural Education.* New York, Social Science Research Council, 1952. 53 p.

Michigan State University, Institute of Research on Overseas Programs. *The International Programs of American Universities: An Inven-*

*tory and Analysis.* East Lansing, Michigan, Michigan State University, 1958. 323 p.

Millbank Memorial Fund. *Modernization Programs in Relation to Human Resources and Population Problems.* New York, 1950. 153 p.

Minnesota, University of. Center for International Relations and Area Studies. *Employment Opportunities for Students Trained in International Relations and Area Studies; a Directory of Governmental and Private Enterprises which Employ Students Trained in International Affairs.* Compiled by Clifton E. Wilson. Minneapolis, Minnesota, 1960. 58 p.

Myers, Charles A. *Labor Problems in the Industrialization of India.* Cambridge, Massachusetts, Harvard University Press, 1958. 297 p.

Myo Htun Lynn, U. *Labour and Labour Movement in Burma.* Rangoon, Department of Economics, University of Rangoon, 1961. 168 p.

Pakistan, Ministry of Labor, Department of Manpower and Employment. *Report of the ILO on the Manpower Survey in Pakistan.* Karachi, 1958. 126 p.

Pakistan, Planning Commission. *The Development and Utilization of Manpower.* Karachi, Government of Pakistan Press, 1960. 18 p.

*Partners for Progress. The ILO's Technical Assistance Program.* Washington, D.C., Washington Branch, International Labor Office (not dated). 63 p.

*Point Four in Bolivia; 1942-1960.* La Paz, Bolivia, United States Operations Mission to Bolivia, 1961. 95 p.

Powesland, P. G. *Economic Policy and Labour; a Study in Uganda's Economic History.* Uganda, East African Institute of Social Research, 1957. 81 p.

*Proposed High-Level Manpower Development of Iran: General Outline and Work Plan.* Washington, Governmental Affairs Institute, 1959. 10 p.

Quattlebaum, Charles A. *Development of Scientific, Engineering and Other Professional Manpower.* 85th Congress, 1st session, House of Representatives, Committee on Education and Labor, Committee Print. Washington, U.S. Government Printing Office, April, 1957. 172 p.

Quattlebaum, Charles Albert and others. *Government Programs in International Education (A Survey and Handbook).* 85th Congress, 2nd session, House Report No. 2712. Forty-second Report by the Committee on Government Operations. Washington, U.S. Government Printing Office, 1959. 251 p.

Raj, K. N. *Employment Aspects of Planning in Underdeveloped Economies.* Cairo, Egypt, National Bank of Egypt. 1957. 46 p.

Rao, Vijendra Kasturi Ranga Varadaraja. *University Education and Em-*

*ployment; a Case Study of Dehli Graduates.* New York, Asia Publishing House, 1961. 45 p.

Romero, Fernando. *Inter-American Cooperation in Vocational Education.* Washington, Pan American Union, Department of Cultural Affairs, Division of Education, 1950. 188 p.

Rosario, Candido V. *Report as a Grantee on Vocational Agriculture.* August 26, 1955, to June 30, 1956, as Philicusa–ICA Grantee; at Oklahoma State University, Stillwater, Oklahoma. Bayombong, Philippines, Nueva Vizcaya Agricultural School (not dated). 35 p.

Scanlon, D. G. *International Education.* New York, Columbia University, Teachers College, 1960. 196 p.

Singh, V. B., and A. K. Saran, editors. *Industrial Labour in India.* New York, Asia Publishing House, 1960. 528 p.

Smith, Bruce L. *Indonesian-American Cooperation in Higher Education.* East Lansing, Michigan, Michigan State University, Institute of Research on Overseas Programs, 1960. 133 p. Bibliography p. 125-130.

Spengler, Joseph J., and Otis D. Duncan. *Demographic Analysis; Selected Readings.* Glencoe, Illinois, The Free Press, 1956. 819 p.

Steinberg, David J., and others. *Cambodia, Its People, Its Society, Its Culture.* New Haven, Connecticut, Yale University Press, 1957. 345 p. (Country Series No. 2.)

*Summary of the Labor Situation in Malaya.* Prepared by the U.S. Department of Labor, Bureau of Labor Statistics. Washington, International Cooperation Administration, Office of Labor Affairs, May, 1958. 20 p. Processed. Selected Bibliography, p. 20.

Sundrum, R. M. *Manpower Resources of Ceylon, 1956-1981.* Colombo, National Planning Council, 1959. 34 p.

Sutton, Francis. *The Ford Foundation Development Program in Africa.* New York, The Ford Foundation, 1961. 10 p.

Tanganyika, Ministry of Education. *Human Resources and Manpower Planning in Tanganyika.* Prepared by The Ford Foundation, J. L. Thurston, Consultant. Dar es Salaam, November, 1960. 30 p. Mimeographed.

*The Technical Assistance Training Program in Education: Annual Report, 1959-60.* U.S. Department of Health, Education and Welfare, Office of Education, Division of International Education, Washington, U.S. Government Printing Office, 1962. 47 p. (OE-14046-60.)

*Technical Cooperation in Industry.* Washington, U.S. Government Printing Office, 1960. 23 p. (U.S. Department of State Publication 7023, Economic Cooperation Series 57.)

Uganda Protectorate, British East Africa, Ministry of Education and Labour. *Report on the Survey of Manpower and Training, July-October 1959.* Prepared by The Ford Foundation in cooperation with the Ministry of Education and Labour, Robert L. Thomas, Consultant, Variously paged. Mimeographed.

United Nations, Department of Public Information. *Helping Economic Development in Asia and the Far East*. New York, United Nations, 1957. 34 p. Technical Training and Assistance, p. 32-34.

United Nations, Department of Social Affairs. *The Determinants and Consequences of Population Trends*. New York, United Nations, 1953. 404 p.

United Nations, Economic Commission for Asia and the Far East. Group of Experts on Programming Techniques. *Formulating Industrial Development Programmes, with Special Reference to Asia and the Far East; Report of the Second Group of Experts on Programming Techniques*. Bangkok, United Nations, Economic Commission for Asia and the Far East, 1961. 137 p.

United Nations, Economic Commission in Latin America. *Progress Report on the Manpower Survey in Latin America*. Bogotá, 1955. 39 p.

U.S. Department of Agriculture, Foreign Agricultural Service. *FAO, Its Organization and Work and United States Participation*. Washington, August, 1960. FAS-M-93. 24 p.

U.S. Department of Labor, Bureau of International Labor Affairs. *Memorandum to Labor Attachés and Other Officers Overseas, on the Subject of Manpower Packet and Manpower Bibliographies*. February 20, 1960. 21 p. Processed.

U.S. Department of Labor, Office of International Labor Affairs. *Technical Cooperation in the Field of Labor. A Prospectus of Consultant Services, Training Programs, Special Services*, Washington (not dated). 29 p.

U.S. Department of State, Office of the Special Assistant to the Secretary for the Coordination of International Educational and Cultural Relations. *Public and Private Association in the International Educational and Cultural Relations of the United States; a Summary Record of Four Conferences Sponsored by the Department of State, 1959-1961*. Washington, 1961. 111 p.

U.S. Department of State. *The Widening Circle. An Account of Public-Private Cooperation in the International Exchange Program of the Department of State*. Washington, U.S. Government Printing Office, 1957. 51 p. (Department of State Publication 6442.)

U.S. International Cooperation Administration. *Technical Cooperation in Education*. Washington, U.S. Government Printing Office, 1960. 31 p. (Department of State Publication No. 7024. Economic Series 58.)

U.S. International Cooperation Administration, Office of Labor Affairs. *Manpower Programs and Planning in Economic Development*. Washington, 1959. 121 p.

Useem, John and Ruth Hill Useem. *The Western-Educated Man in India:*

*a Study of His Social Roles and Influence*. New York, Dryden Press, 1955. 237 p.

Ward, Barbara. *India and the West*. New York, W. W. Norton and Co., Inc., 1961. 256 p. Chapter 12, The Indian Plans, p. 153-194.

————, *The Interplay of East and West; Points of Conflict and Cooperation*. New York, W. W. Norton and Co., Inc., 1957. 152 p.

Warmbrunn, Werner. *Observations of Education and International Exchange in Asia. A Report of a Study Trip, September to December, 1960*. New York, National Association of Foreign Student Advisers, 1961. 30 p. (NAFSA studies and papers. Professional grant report No. 4.)

Werts, Leo R. *A Manpower Program for Economic Development and Observations and Suggestions Concerning India's Manpower Program*. India Ministry of Home Affairs, Directorate of Manpower, New Delhi, December, 1960. 153 p. Mimeographed.

Wilson, Howard E. "Education as an Implement of International Cooperation." *International Conciliation*, November, 1945. No. 415. New York, Carnegie Endowment for International Peace, 1945, p. 707-721.

Woodman, Dorothy. *The Republic of Indonesia*. London, Cressett Press, 1955. 444 p.

Younger, Kenneth Gilmour. *The Public Services in New States; a Study in Some Trained Manpower Problems*. London, New York, Oxford University Press, 1960. 113 p.

## 3. Articles in Periodicals

Al-Arabi, M. "A Modern Apprenticeship Scheme in the United Arab Republic." Geneva, *International Labour Review*, v. 84, December, 1961, p. 478-498.

"An Agriculture Committee Statement: Facilitating International Agricultural Research and Education." Washington, *Looking Ahead*, v. 8, May, 1960, p. 1-4.

"Answer to Questions on Technical Assistance." New York, *United Nations Review*, April, 1958, p. 24-32.

Barton, E. D. "Global Careers: A Program." New York, Institute of International Education, London, *Overseas*, v. 1, January, 1962, p. 7-10.

Berg, Sherwood O. "University Training in Agricultural Economics for Foreign Students." Menasha, Wisconsin, *Journal of Farm Economics*, v. 41, December, 1959, p. 1373-1383.

Berol, Suzanne W. "Brazilian Hires UN Technical Assistance Experts for Latin America." Boston, Massachusetts, *Christian Science Monitor*, February 13, 1962, p. 5.

Bodenman, Paul S. "Educational Cooperation with Foreign Countries." Washington, *Higher Education*, v. IX, No. 13, March 1, 1953, p. 145-150.

Brewer, Sam P. "U.N. Special Fund Will Stress Training in New Aid Projects." New York, *New York Times*, January 12, 1962, p. 6.

Brooks, J. J. "Overseas Schools: Crucibles of International Education." New York, Columbia University, *Teachers College Record*, v. 63, October, 1961, p. 14-18.

Buchanan, Mark T. "Land-grant Education Comes to Pakistan." Pullman, Washington, *Washington State Review*, v. 5, spring, 1962, p. 20-23.

Caldwell, O. J. "International Education Activities of the Office of Education." Washington, *Higher Education*, v. 12, September, 1955, p. 4-6.

Carpenter, Howard S. "Manpower in Developing Countries." Washington, *Employment Security Review*, May, 1960, p. 3-6.

Carr, William George, editor. "International Frontiers in Education." Philadelphia, *Annals of the American Academy of Political and Social Science*, v. 235, September, 1944, 180 p.

Carter, W. D. "UNESCO's Exchange of Persons Program." New York, Institute of International Education, *IIE News Bulletin*, v. 32, November, 1956, p. 10-13.

Clark, Neil M. "Campus Ambassadors." Philadelphia, *Saturday Evening Post*, v. 221, May 7, 1949, p. 38-39, 180-183.

Clay, Robert J. "The Employment Service and Manpower Planning in Peru." Washington, *Employment Security Review*, May, 1960, p. 20-24.

Cleveland, Harlan. "The Overseas Americans: Agenda for Action." New York, Institute of International Education, *IIE Bulletin*, v. 35, March, 1960, p. 13-21.

Conclaves de Souza, Joa. "Skills for Tomorrow." Washington, *Americas*, v. 13, December, 1961, p. 5-8.

Darrah, L. B. "Preparing Foreign Students to Study Farm Economic Problems in Their Own Countries." Menasha, Wisconsin, *Journal of Farm Economics*, v. 41, December, 1959, p. 1384-1392.

Datar, B. N. "Manpower Planning in India." Geneva, *International Labour Review*, July, 1958, p. 56-70.

"The Development of Vocational Guidance in Asia." Geneva, *International Labour Review*, v. 78, December, 1958, p. 585-602.

Dunlop, John T. and Melvin Rothbaum. "International Comparisons of Wage Structure." Geneva, *International Labour Review*, April, 1955, p. 3-19.

Duttweiler, Gottlieb. "New Aid Medium: Cadre, Not Money." Boston, *Christian Science Monitor*, March 18, 1960, p. 10.

"East-West Link Rising in Hawaii. Center's First Buildings Due for Use in September." New York, *New York Times,* May 13, 1962, p. 83.

"Economic Motivations and Stimulations in Underdeveloped Countries." Paris, UNESCO, *International Social Science Bulletin,* v. VI, No. 3, 1954, p. 369-476.

"Education in Africa." New York, *United Nations Review,* v. 8, July, 1961, p. 27-28.

Fei, Edward. "Programs for Pakistan." London, *Overseas,* v. 1, December, 1961, p. 20-25.

Fischlowitz, Istanislau. "Manpower Problems and Prospects in Latin America." Washington, *Monthly Labor Review,* September, 1960, p. 909-916.

Fulbright Program Issue. New York, Institute of International Education, *IIE News Bulletin,* v. 35, April, 1960, p. 2-46.

Gailer, John W. "And in Africa?" London, *Technical Education,* v. 3, January, 1961, p. 14-17.

George, W. F. "Vocational Education, a Major Hope for the Victory of Freedom." Washington, *American Vocational Journal,* v. 31, December, 1956, p. 5-6.

Hanna, Paul R. "Education as an Economic and Social Instrument in the Newly Developing Nations." Bloomington, Indiana, *Phi Delta Kappan,* v. 43, May, 1962, p. 354-356.

"Helping Overseas." London, *Times Educational Supplement,* v. 2434, January 12, 1962, p. 51.

Hinman, E. Harold and Clifford A. Pease. "International Assistance in Medical Education." Chicago, *Journal of Medical Education,* v. 36, September, 1961, p. 1042-51.

Howell, M. D. "Helping Hand for a Friendly Nation." New York, Institute of International Education, *IIE News Bulletin,* v. 35, November, 1959, p. 4-11.

"Human Resources Planning: Aid to Free World Development." Washington, *Employment Security Review,* May, 1960, p. 3-24.

International Labor Organization. "Assignment in Tripoli: ILO's Training Centre." London, *Times Educational Supplement,* v. 2300, June 19, 1959, p. 1123.

"International Labour Standards and Asian Countries." Geneva, *International Labour Review,* v. 83, April, 1961, p. 303-321.

Jackson, Lowell. "Center for East-West Cultural and Technical Exchange." New York, *School and Society,* v. 89, October 21, 1961, p. 349-350.

Jeffries, C. "Job Overseas." London, *Times Educational Supplement* 2304, July 17, 1959, p. VIII.

Jones, Ronald W. "Personnel Management for Technical Cooperation." Philadelphia, *The Annals of the American Academy of Political and Social Science,* v. 323, May, 1959, p. 100-110.

Kandel, I. L. "Comparative Education and Underdeveloped Countries: A New Dimension." New York, *Comparative Education Review*, v. 4, February, 1961, p. 130-135.

Kerr, Clark, and others. "The Labor Problem in Economic Development: Framework for Reappraisal." Geneva, *International Labour Review*, March, 1955, p. 223-235.

Kimble, George H. T. "Compelling Needs—Education for Africans." New York, *New York Times Magazine*, March 5, 1961, p. 31, 90-91.

Lederer, William J. and Eugene Burdick. "Salute to Deeds of Non-Ugly Americans." New York, *Life*, v. 47, no. 23, December 7, 1959, p. 148-163, intermittent.

Lengyel, Peter. "Investment in Education: Notes on Criteria for the Determination of Policies." New York, *UNESCO Chronicle*, v. VII, no. 4, April, 1961, p. 113.

Lewis, A. B. "Training Students of Less Developed Countries in Agricultural Economics." Menasha, Wisconsin, *Journal of Farm Economics*, v. 41, December, 1959, p. 1363-1372.

Lewis, W. Arthur. "Economic Development with Unlimited Supplies of Labour." Manchester, England, *The Manchester School of Economic and Social Studies*, May, 1954, p. 139-191.

———, "Needs of New States—Science, Men and Money." Chicago, *Bulletin of the Atomic Scientists*, v. 17, February, 1961, p. 43-47.

Liebstein, Harvey. "The Theory of Underemployment in Backward Countries." Chicago, *Journal of Political Economy*, April, 1957, p. 91-103.

Littell, Robert. "They're Helping Greeks to Help Themselves." Pleasantville, New York, *Reader's Digest*, v. 77, September, 1960, p. 129-134.

Lodge, George C. "Labor's Role in Newly Developing Countries." New York, *Foreign Affairs*, v. 37, July, 1959, p. 658-671.

Malti, Michel G. "Technical Education and Research in India." Ithaca, New York, *Cornell Engineers*, v. 26, January, 1961, p. 12-16, 35-37.

"Manpower Aspects of the Lower Mekong Basin Development Project." Geneva, *International Labour Review*, v. 85, April, 1962, p. 357-367.

Mathur, V. S. "Workers' Education in Asia: The Experience of the Asian Trade Union College of the I.C.F.T.U." Geneva, *International Labour Review*, v. 83, June, 1961, p. 554-575.

Mobley, M. D. "Pakistan: First Line of Defense." Washington, *American Vocational Journal*, v. 32, December, 1957, p. 23+.

Moran, H. O. "Canada's Educational Aid Program." Toronto, *Canadian Education and Research Digest*, v. 1, December, 1961, p. 5-12.

Myers, Charles A. "Labour Problems of Rationalisation: The Experience of India." Geneva, *International Labour Review*, v. 73, May, 1956, p. 431-450.

Neyland, Leedell W. "Africa: New Frontier for Teaching in Negro Institutions of Higher Learning." Washington, *Educational Record,* v. 43, January, 1961, p. 57-61.

Niculescu, B. M. "Recruitment of Foreign Staff for Newly Developing Countries." Brussels, *Civilisations,* v. 10, no. 1, 1960, p. 13-24.

"The Organization of Employment Services in Economically Underdeveloped Countries." Geneva, *International Labour Review,* April, 1956, p. 315-333.

Pastro, Jerome K. "The Role of Farm Management in Underdeveloped Countries." Menasha, Wisconsin, *Journal of Farm Economics,* v. 43, August, 1961, p. 606-615.

Pereira, Juan. "Bolivia's Industrial Schools." Washington, *Americas,* v. 9, May, 1956, p. 21-25.

Porter, Sylvia, "Europe Shows the Way." *Washington Star,* May 7, 1962, p. A-14.

Rens, Jef. "Helping the Andean Indians." Washington, *AFL-CIO American Federationist,* April, 1958, p. 16-19.

———, "Vocational Training and the Establishment of Service Workshops in a Poor Rural Area. The Experience of the Andean Indian Programme." Geneva, *International Labour Review,* v. 85, February, 1962, p. 3-147.

"Report on an International Conference on Vocational Training." Geneva, *International Labour Review,* v. 75, May, 1957, p. 450-467.

Robinson, J. H. "Operation Cross-roads Africa." New York, Institute of International Education, *IIE News Bulletin,* v. 36, March, 1961, p. 9-12.

Rosen, Howard. "Technicians in the Labor Force of Russia and America." Washington, *Monthly Labor Review,* v. 81, January, 1958, p. 1-5.

Rossignol, E. "The Vocational Training of Adults." Geneva, *International Labour Review,* v. 76, October, 1957, p. 325-348.

Ruffner, R. W. "Technical Cooperation in Education through the International Cooperation Administration." Washington, *Higher Education,* v. 16, April, 1960, p. 7-12.

Samuels, Gertrude. "In Answer to Africa's Need for Teachers." New York, *New York Times Magazine,* March 18, 1962, p. 89-90, 92, 94.

———, "To Meet Africa's Great Need—Education." New York, *New York Times Magazine,* August 20, 1961, p. 33-34, 38.

Scanlon, David G. "African Education." New York, *Saturday Review,* v. 44, August 19, 1961, p. 34-35, 50-52.

Schiller, Herbert I. "The United States and the Educational Needs of the Developing Economies." Urbana, Illinois, University of Illinois, *Quarterly Review of Economics and Business,* v. 2, February, 1962, p. 31-38.

Schultz, Theodore W. "Capital Formation by Education." Chicago, *Journal of Political Economy,* v. 68, No. 6, December, 1960, p. 571-583.

———, "U.S. Endeavors to Assist Low-Income Countries Improve Economic Capabilities of Their People." Menasha, Wisconsin, *Journal of Farm Economics,* v. 43, December, 1961, p. 1068-1077. Discussion by Anthony M. Traug, p. 1077-1080.

"Science at Work in the Thai Jungle. Role of FAO in Expanding Thailand's Food Output." New York, *United Nations Review,* v. 3, February, 1957, p. 45-48.

"Selection and Training of Vocational Guidance Personnel: I." Geneva, *International Labour Review,* v. 77, May, 1958, p. 469-480.

"Selection and Training of Vocational Guidance Personnel: II." Geneva, *International Labour Review,* v. 77, June, 1958, p. 565-580.

Shane, Harold G. "Our Campus: The World." Washington, *NEA Journal,* v. 50, May, 1961, p. 16-18.

Shuster, George N. "Report on the UN (Pt. 2); The Trials and Triumph of UNESCO." New York, *Saturday Review,* v. 45, February 24, 1962, p. 21-22, 63.

Sinclair, Adelaide. "The World's Deprived Children." Washington, *Children,* v. 9, March-April, 1962, p. 84-88.

Spaull, Hebe. "Africa Needs Self-Made Men." London, *New Commonwealth,* v. 39, June, 1961, p. 365-367.

"Special Fund—48 Projects Approved for 38 Countries." New York, *United Nations Review,* v. 9, February, 1962, p. 14-16.

"Special Fund Projects Under Way in Thirteen Countries." New York, *United Nations Review,* July, 1959, p. 10-17.

Storm, William B. and Richard N. Gable. "Technical Assistance in Higher Education: An Iranian Illustration." Washington, *The Educational Record,* v. 41, no. 2, April, 1960, p. 175-182.

Strother, Robert S. "Low-Budget Miracle in Foreign Aid." Pleasantville, New York, *Reader's Digest,* v. 76, no. 453, January, 1960, p. 165-169.

Suffridge, James A. "The Urgent Needs of Asian Workers." Washington, *AFL-CIO American Federationist,* July, 1961, p. 10-14.

Teltsch, Kathleen. "UN Lures Many from Retirement." New York, *New Times,* February 14, 1960, p. 17.

Van Eerde, Katharine S. "Problems and Alignments in African Labor." New York, *Social Research,* v. 29, spring, 1962, p. 73-100.

Van der Kroef, Justus M. "Asia's Educated Unemployed." London, *Eastern World,* v. 15, November, 1961, p. 16-17.

"Vocational and Technical Education: Reviews of the Literature for the Six-Year Period Since October 1950." Washington, *Review of Educational Research,* v. 26, October, 1956, p. 349-410.

Watson, Adam. "Problems of Adjustment in the Middle East." Philadelphia, *Annals of the American Academy of Political and Social Science,* v. 282, July, 1952, p. 60-63.

Willis, Benjamin C. "Adult Education in the World Community." Washington, *School Life,* v. 44, no. 5, March, 1962, p. 5-8.

Wit, Daniel. "Personnel Problems Facing Firms in Southeast Asia." Bloomington, Indiana, *Business Horizons,* fall, 1960, p. 77-83.

"The World's Working Population: Its Distribution by Status and Occupation." Geneva, *International Labour Review,* v. 74, August, 1956, p. 174-192.

"The World's Working Population: Its Industrial Distribution." Geneva, *International Labour Review,* v. 73, May, 1956, p. 501-521.

## II. VOLUNTARY SERVICE PROGRAMS

### 1. Books and Pamphlets

Adams, Richard Neinbold. *United States University Cooperation in Latin America, a Study Based on Selected Programs in Bolivia, Chile, Peru and Mexico by Richard N. Adams and Charles C. Cumberland.* East Lansing, Michigan, Institute of Research on Overseas Programs, Michigan State University, 1960. 264 p.

Albertson, Maurice L., and others. *New Frontiers for American Youth: Perspective on the Peace Corps.* Washington, Public Affairs Press, 1961. 212 p.

Albertson, Maurice L., Pauline E. Birky, and Andrew E. Rice. *Final Report: The Peace Corps.* Fort Collins, Colorado, Colorado State University Research Foundation, 1961. Various paging.

———, *Preliminary Report: A Youth Corps for Service Abroad.* Fort Collins, Colorado, Colorado State University Research Foundation, 1961. 26 p.

*American Friends Service Committee. 40 Years of Service.* Philadelphia, American Friends Service Committee, 1957. 12 p.

American Institute for Research, Pittsburgh, Pennsylvania, Institute for International Services. *Working Effectively Overseas* (by) Paul Spector and Harley O. Preston. Prepared for the Peace Corps. Washington, 1961. 179 p.

Book, E. A. *Fifty Years of Technical Assistance. Some Administrative Experiences of U.S. Voluntary Agencies.* Chicago, Public Administration Clearing House, 1954. 65 p.

Collison, W. N., editor. *Directory of American Voluntary and Non-profit Agencies Interested in Technical Assistance.* New York, American Council of Voluntary Agencies for Foreign Service, 1958. Unpaged.

Committee on Educational Interchange Policy. *College and University Programs of Academic Exchange; Suggestions for the Study of Exchanges of Students, Faculty and Short-term Visitors.* New York, 1960. 36 p.

*Executive Director's Report.* Washington, International Voluntary Services, Inc., April 15, 1962. 8 p. (Processed.)

*Final Report, National Conference on Youth Service Abroad.* Philadelphia, United States National Student Association, 1961. 40 p.

Freeman, A. V. *Government Utilization of Private Agencies in Technical Assistance.* Washington, U.S. Government Printing Office, 1956. 46 p.

Glover, Robert Hall. *The Progress of World-wide Missions.* Rev. and enl. by J. Herbert Kane. New York, Harper, 1960. 502 p.

Hayes, Samuel P. *An International Peace Corps.* Washington, Public Affairs Institute, 1961. 96 p. Appendix: Principal Private Organizations Already Carrying on International Service Programs in Which Young American Volunteers Participate, p. 95-96.

Hoopes, Roy H. *The Complete Peace Corps Guide.* Introduction by R. Sargent Shriver. New York, Dial Press, 1961. 180 p.

*ICA and U.S. Voluntary Agencies.* Washington, U.S. International Cooperation Administration, June, 1959. 22 p.

Institute of International Education. *The Institute of International Education, 1919-1944: Its Aims and Achievements During Twenty-five Years.* New York, The Institute, 1944. 40 p.

*International Farm Youth Exchange.* Washington, National 4-H Club Foundation, 1960. 6 p.

*International Voluntary Services, Vietnam. Annual Report,* June, 1960-June, 1961. Washington, International Voluntary Services, Inc., 1961. 45 p.

*International Voluntary Services.* Washington, International Voluntary Services, Inc., 3 p. (not dated.)

Isaacs, Harold R. *Emergent Americans: A Report on "Crossroads Africa."* New York, The John Day Company, 1962. 158 p.

Kinkead, Katharine T. *Walk Together, Talk Together; The American Field Service, Student Exchange Program.* New York, W. W. Norton, 1962. 101 p.

*The Koinonia Foundation.* Baltimore, Maryland, The Koinonia Foundation. 24 p. (not dated.)

Maddox, J. G. *Technical Assistance by Religious Agencies in Latin America.* Chicago, University of Chicago Press, 1956. 139 p.

National Conference on Youth Service Abroad, Washington, 1961. *Final Report.* Philadelphia, U.S. National Student Association, 1961. 40 p.

*Neighborhood Is in the Heart.* Oklahoma City, World Neighbors, Inc. 7 p. (not dated.)

*Peace Corps Fact Book.* Washington, Peace Corps, 1961, 28 p.

*Peace Corps Profiles. Description of the First 9 Projects.* Washington, Peace Corps, November 1, 1961. 30 p.

Pickett, Clarence E. *For More Than Bread. An Autobiographical Account of Twenty-two Years' Work with the American Friends Service Committee.* Boston, Little Brown and Company, 1953. 433 p.

*Planning and Management of Development Programs for Private and Public Organizations.* New York, International Development Services, Inc., 1962. 12 p.

Ravenholt, Albert. *The Peace Corps in the Philippines.* New York, American Universities Field Staff, Inc., 1962. 12 p. (Southeast Asia Series, v. X, no. 9.)

*The Role of Voluntary Agencies in Technical Assistance.* New York, American Council of Voluntary Agencies for Foreign Service, 1958. 176 p.

Russell, Daniel. *As a Volunteer.* Washington, International Voluntary Services, Inc., 8 p. (not dated.)

Savord, Ruth. *American Agencies Interested in International Affairs.* New York, Council on Foreign Relations. 1942. 199 p.

Shriver, Sargent. *Summary of Report to the President on the Peace Corps.* Washington, Office of the White House Press Secretary, 1961. 12 p.

Taft, Charles P. *Status Report—Voluntary Agency Participation in Technical Cooperation Programs.* Washington, International Cooperation Administration. April 15, 1957. Memorandum. 7 p. Processed.

*Training for Overseas Service.* Baltimore, Maryland, Koinonia Foundation. 16 p. (not dated.)

*UNRWA-VID Project Statement.* Springfield, Massachusetts, Volunteers for International Development, Inc., 1962. 5 p. Processed.

U.S. Congress. Conference Committees, 1961. Peace Corps Act; Conference Report to Accompany H.R. 7500. Washington, U.S. Government Printing Office, 1961. 23 p. (87th Congress, 1st session. House. Report no. 1239.)

U.S. Congress. House. Committee on Foreign Affairs. *Amending the Peace Corps Act; Report . . . on H.R. 10700, to Amend the Peace Corps Act.* Washington, U.S. Government Printing Office, 1962. 42 p. (87th Congress, 2nd session. House. Report no. 1470.)

————, Peace Corps Act Amendments. *Hearings, 87th Congress, 2nd session on H.R. 10404, a Bill to Amend the Peace Corps Act.* March 1, 6, 7, and 8, 1962. Washington, U.S. Government Printing Office, 1962. 169 p.

————, *The Peace Corps. Hearings, Eighty-seventh Congress, first session, on H.R. 7500, a Bill to Provide for a Peace Corps to Help the Peoples of Interested Countries and Areas in Meeting Their Needs for Skilled Manpower.* Washington, U.S. Government Printing

Office, 1961. 78 p. (87th Congress, 1st session. House. Report no. 1115.)

U.S. Congress. Senate. Committee on Foreign Relations. *Peace Corps Act Amendments. Hearings, 87th Congress, 2nd session; on S. 2935, a Bill to Amend the Peace Corps.*

——, *Peace Corps Act Amendments. Report to Accompany S. 2935.* Washington, U.S. Government Printing Office, 1962. 28 p. (87th Congress, 2nd session. Senate. Report no. 1325.)

——, *The Peace Corps. Hearings, 87th Congress, 1st session, on S. 2000, a Bill to Provide for a Peace Corps to Help the Peoples of Interested Countries and Areas in Meeting Their Needs for Skilled Manpower; June 22 and 23, 1961. Washington, U. S. Government* Printing Office, 1961. 254 p.

——, *The Peace Corps. Report . . . on S. 2000.* Washington, U.S. Government Printing Office, 1961. 24 p. (87th Congress, 1st session. Senate. Report no. 706.)

U.S. Department of State. Bureau of Educational and Cultural Affairs. *International Educational, Cultural and Related Activities for African Countries South of the Sahara.* Washington, U.S. Government Printing Office, 1961. 321 p.

U.S. Department of State. External Research Division. *African Programs of U.S. Organizations; a Selective Directory.* Washington, U.S. Govment Printing Office, 1961. 90 p.

U.S. Laws, Statutes, etc. *An Act to Provide for a Peace Corps to Help the Peoples of Interested Countries and Areas in Meeting Their Needs for Skilled Manpower.* Washington, U.S. Government Printing Office, 1961. 16 p.

U.S. National Student Association. *Fourteenth Annual National Student Congress Working Papers.* University of Wisconsin, August 20-August 30, 1961. Philadelphia, 1961. Various pagings.

U.S. Peace Corps. *Peace Corps Volunteers.* Washington, 1961. Various pagings.

U.S. President, 1961 (Kennedy). *Establishment of Permanent Peace Corps. Message from the President of the United States Transmitting Special Message for the Establishment of a Permanent Peace Corps.* Washington, U.S. Government Printing Office, 1961. 4 p. (87th Congress, 1st session. House. Document no. 98.)

U.S. Treaties, etc., 1961 (Kennedy). *Peace Corps Program. Agreement between the United States of American and Ghana Effected by Exchange of Notes Signed at Accra July 19, 1961.* Washington, U.S. Government Printing Office, 1961. 5 p.

——, *Agreement Between the United States of America and Malaya Effected by Exchange of Notes Signed at Kuala Lumpur September 4, 1961.* Washington, U.S. Government Printing Office, 1961. 4 p.

*Volunteers for International Development in Action.* Springfield, Massachusetts, Volunteers for International Development, Inc. (not dated). 5 p.

*A World at Peace; A World in Peril: The Decision Is Yours.* Oklahoma City, World Neighbors, Inc. (not dated). 3 p.

Wingenbach, Charles E. *The Peace Corps; Who, How and Where.* With a Foreword by Hubert H. Humphrey. New York, John Day Co., 1961. 154 p.

Zwayer, Wayland. *Directory of American Voluntary and Non-profit Agencies Interested in Technical Assistance.* New York, American Council of Voluntary Agencies for Foreign Service, Inc., 1960. 217 p.

Zwayer, Wayland, editor. Technical Assistance Information Clearing House. *American Voluntary and Non-profit Agencies in Technical Assistance Abroad; a Summary.* New York, American Council of Voluntary Agencies for Foreign Service, 1961. 226 p.

## 2. Articles in Periodicals

"A Stronger British Corps for Peace." London, *Times,* May 26, 1962, p. 9.

Abiko, Nobuo. "Youthful Aide to Nigeria." Boston, *Christian Science Monitor,* May 3, 1962, p. 1.

"Aid Volunteers Sought. Private Group Calls for 50 to Help in UN Program." New York, *New York Times,* October 23, 1960, p. 33.

"As Visiting Statesmen See Our Schools." Chicago, *Nation's Schools,* v. 67, June, 1961, p. 51-56.

Barkin, Solomon. "Full Employment on a World-Wide Scale." New York, *Challenge,* v. 10, June, 1962, p. 37-40.

Barlow, R. M. "Peace Corps Revisited." New York, *America,* v. 106, October 7, 1961, p. 16-18.

Bayley, Edwin R. "The View from Inside the Peace Corps." Madison, Wisconsin, *Progressive,* v. 25, September, 1961, p. 27-30.

Belshaw, Michael, and Franklin Wallick. "Would a Peace Corps Be Useful?" New York, *Foreign Policy Bulletin,* v. 40, January 15, 1961, p. 68-70.

Boyer, William Harrison. "Proposed: A Vast Expansion of High-School Student Exchange." Bloomington, Indiana, *Phi Delta Kappan,* v. 43, May, 1962, p. 357-359.

Braestrup, Peter. "Peace Corpsman No. 1.—A Progress Report." New York, *New York Times Magazine,* December 17, 1961, p. 11, 64-66.

Breed, Joseph B. "The Unofficial Ambassadors, USA." New York, *The Magazine of American Affairs,* v. II, no. 5, November, 1952, p. 56-62.

Brice, Edward Warner. "Operation Export." New York, *Overview,* v. 2, January, 1961, p. 40-43.

Brickman, W. W. "Peace Corps and Educational Competence." New York, *School and Society,* v. 89, March 25, 1961, p. 135.

Bryan, Robert S. "Opportunities for Service in the Peace Corps." Washington, *Occupational Outlook Quarterly,* v. 5, September, 1961, p. 11-15.

*Busy Young Americans Around the World: Up Front with the Peace Corps.* New York, *Life,* v. 52, January 5, 1962, p. 19-25.

"Careers in World Affairs: With a Salute to the Peace Corps." New York, World Affairs Center for the United States, *Intercom,* v. 3, no. 2, April, 1961, p. 12-63.

"Churches Change Aid in Taiwan." Washington, *Post,* May 9, 1962, p. A-7.

"Countries Triple Requests for Peace Corps Teachers." Washington, *The School Administrator,* v. 19, no. 9, June, 1962, p. 3.

DeMott, Benjamin. "The Peace Corps' 'Secret Mission.'" New York, *Harper's Magazine,* v. 223, September, 1961, p. 63-67.

Dennis, L. E. "Peace Corps: A New Dimension of Public Service." Washington, *Higher Education,* v. 17, May, 1961, p. 3-5.

——, "Training of Peace Corps Volunteers." Washington, *Higher Education,* v. 17, May, 1961, p. 6-10.

Dickson, A. "Voluntary Service Overseas." London, *Times Educational Supplement 2376,* December 2, 1960, sup. XIV.

Dickson, Alec. "Pioneers Overseas." London, *Overseas,* v. 1, April, 1962, p. 11-16.

——, "Voluntary Service Overseas." London, *Times Educational Supplement,* December 7, 1960, p. XIV.

"Directory of Voluntary Organizations in World Affairs." New York, Foreign Policy Association-World Affairs Center, *Intercom,* v. 3, no. 3, May, 1961, p. 12-54.

Dole, Kenneth. "Church Aid Credited for Progress in Nigeria." Washington, *Post,* May 29, 1962, p. B4.

Doyle, Anne. "Nurses in the Peace Corps." Service Publishing, Inc., Nantucket, Rhode Island, *Tomorrow's Nurses,* v. 2, December-January 1961-62, p. 6-7.

Dunne, George H., and C. J. McNaspy. "How We Look to Others." New York, *America,* v. 105, May 13, 1961, p. 272-275.

Eckelberry, R. H. "Practical Idealism." Columbus, Ohio, *Educational Research Bulletin,* v. 40, May, 1961, p. 126-7.

Erb, Mary Barclay. "Peace Corps . . . A Pied Piper Scheme." Concord, New Hampshire, *American Mercury,* v. 92, June, 1961, p. 60-64.

"Expatriatism Is Not Enough." London, *The Economist,* April 21, 1962, p. 226-227. Representative List of Organizations Assisting Overseas Service, p. 227.

"Focus on Giving and Sharing." New York, World Affairs Center for the United States, *Intercom,* v. 1, no. 10, December, 1959-January, 1960, p. 14-26.

Greenfield, Meg. "How to Be an American Abroad—and Get Away With It." New York, *Reporter*, v. 25, December 7, 1961, p. 36-39.

Hatcher, H. "Conference Considers Youth Corps Ideas." Washington, *Journal of Home Economics*, v. 53, February, 1961, p. 124-5.

———, "Peace Corps and Exchange Program Discussed." Washington, *Journal of Home Economics*, v. 53, May, 1961, p. 397.

Higdon, Hal. "*International Healers of Body and Soul*." Chicago, *Today's Health*, v. 39, May, 1961, p. 22-25, 69-72.

Hoopes, Roy. "Peace Corps: One Year After." Washington, *Foreign Service Journal*, v. 39, January, 1962, p. 36-39, 42.

Humphrey, Hubert H. "How the Youth Peace Corps Will Work." Washington, *This Week*, April 2, 1961, p. 4-5.

———, "Peace Corps Act. Remarks in the Senate." Washington, *Congressional Record* (daily edition), v. 107, June 1, 1961, p. 8660-8675.

———, "The Peace Corps on Trial." Chicago, *PTA Magazine*, v. 55, May, 1961, p. 4-6.

"International Organizations." New York, Institute of International Education, *IIE News Bulletin*, v. 36, April, 1961, p. 12-37.

Kennedy, John F. "Special Message on the Peace Corps from the President to the Congress of the United States." March 1, 1961. Washington, *Higher Education*, v. 17, May, 1961, p. 10-11.

Magee, Raymond J. "Volunteers for International Development." Washington, *International Development Review*, v. II, no. 2, October, 1960, p. 34.

Mill, Edward M. "In the Service of the Nation." New York, Long Island University, *LIU News*, April, 1961, 2 p.

"More Than Conquerors." Chicago, *Time*, v. 75, April 18, 1960, p. 64-76.

"New Developments Overseas." Oklahoma City, World Neighbors, Inc., *World Neighbors Newsletter*, v. 10, no. 1, March, 1962, p. 1-4.

Nugent, John P. "The Peace Corps Comes to Tanganyika." New York, *Reporter*, v. 26, February 1, 1962, p. 35-36.

Otten, Alan L. "Peace Corps Switch." New York, *Wall Street Journal*, v. 157, June 22, 1961, p. 1, 11.

"Outward Bound Head." London, *Times Educational Supplement*, v. 2408, July 14, 1961, p. 54.

Kimble, George H. T. "Challenges to the Peace Corps." New York, *New York Times Magazine*, May 14, 1961, p. 9, 98-100.

" 'Peace Corps' Aids Venezuelans. 30 in a Private Group Working in Villages." New York, *New York Times*, May 13, 1962, p. 45.

"Peace Corps Established." London, *Times Educational Supplement*, v. 2390, March 10, 1961, p. 466.

"Peace Corps to Stay; Girl May Resign." London, *Times Educational Supplement*, v. 2422, October 20, 1961, p. 509.

Pollock, J. C. "Missions and Governments in Asia To-day." Nashville, Tennessee, *Quarterly Review,* January, 1961, p. 31-43.

"Proposal for the Establishment of an International Youth Service: Committee on Educational Interchange Policy." New York, *Institute of International Education News Bulletin,* v. 36, February, 1961, p. 27-30.

"Quakers Running Own Peace Corps in 8 Lands. Young Volunteers Helping on Health and Social Work." New York, *New York Times,* May 13, 1962, p. 46.

"Queen Receives Volunteers; Competition from Peace Corps." London, *Times Educational Supplement,* v. 2409, September 29, 1961, p. 384.

Reuss, Henry S. "A Progress Report on the Point 4 Youth Corps." Speech in the House. Washington, *Congressional Record* (daily edition), v. 107, January 10, 1961, p. A159-A160.

———, "Some Roots of the Peace Corps." Remarks in the House. Washington, *Congressional Record* (daily edition), v. 107, June 5, 1961, p. 8824-8826.

———, "Youth for Peace." Madison, Wisconsin, *Progressive,* v. 25, February, 1961, p. 16-18.

———, "Youth for Peace." Washington, *Social Education,* v. 25, April, 1961, p. 175-7.

Rusk, Dean. "Building the Frontiers of Freedom." Washington, *Department of State Bulletin,* v. 44, June 19, 1961, p. 947-955.

Samuels, Gertrude. "A Force of Youth as a Force for Peace." New York, *New York Times Magazine,* February 5, 1961, p. 947-955.

Schanche, Don A. "An American Hero." Philadelphia, *The Saturday Evening Post,* v. 235, June 2, 1962, p. 15-20.

Sennholz, Hans F. "Volunteers for the Peace Corps." Orange, Connecticut, *Freeman,* v. 11, September, 1961, p. 38-43.

Shaffer, Helen B. "Government Youth Corps." Washington, *Editorial Research Reports,* v. 1, no. 1, 1961, p. 3-20.

Shapp, Milton J. "The Role of the Peace Corps in America's Foreign Program. In Extension of Remarks of Herman Toll." Washington, *Congressional Record* (daily edition), v. 107, October 3, 1961, p. A7934-A7935.

Shriver, Sargent. "Teachers and the Peace Corps." Chicago, *American Teacher Magazine,* v. 46, October, 1961, p. 7-8.

———, "The Peace Corps and Private Agencies." New York, Foreign Policy Association-World Affairs Center, *Intercom,* v. 3, no. 2, April, 1961, p. 1.

———, "Peace Corps Vistas." New York, Institute of International Education, *Overseas,* v. 1, December, 1961, p. 2-5.

———, "Peace Corps: Trial Balance—One Year Later." New York, *Saturday Review,* v. 45, May 19, 1962, p. 22-23, 49.

Sims, A. G. "Wanted: A Certain Quality of Free Enterprise." New York, Institute of International Education, *Overseas,* v. 1, September, 1961, p. 11-13.

Smoot, Dan. "Youth Peace Corps." Dallas, Texas, *Dan Smoot Report,* v. 7, March 13, 1961, p. 81-88.

Sokolsky, George E., and R. Sargent Shriver. "Can the Peace Corps Do the Job?" New York, *Saturday Review,* v. 44, June 17, 1961, p. 17-19, 54.

Stoerker, C. F. "Church's Peace Corps." New York, *International Journal of Religious Education,* v. 37, June, 1961, p. 4-6.

———, "Service Is a Universal Language." New York, *International Journal of Religious Education,* v. 36, November, 1959, p. 26-27.

Stoerker, C. Frederick. "The Peace Corps in Perspective." Chicago, *The Christian Century,* v. LXXVIII, April 12, 1961, p. 450-452.

Stone, D. C. "Peace Corps: Caveats." New York, Institute of International Education, *Overseas,* v. 1, December, 1961, p. 6-10.

U.S. Peace Corps. "The Need for the Peace Corps." In remarks of Senator H. H. Humphrey. Washington, *Congressional Record* (daily edition), v. 107, August 23, 1961, p. 15725-15731.

"U.S. Proposes Volunteer Corps to Aid UNESCO." Washington, *Post,* July 21, 1961, p. A-1.

"Voluntary Agencies." New York, World Affairs Center for the United States, *Intercom,* v. 2, no. 1, February, 1960, p. 21-28.

"What Teachers Should Know About the Peace Corps." Washington, *NEA Journal,* v. 50, May, 1961, p. 26.

"Winant Volunteers; Colorado to Bethnal Green." London, *Times Educational Supplement,* v. 2149, July 27, 1956, p. 983.

## III. SOCIAL AND ECONOMIC DEVELOPMENT

### 1. Bibliographies

*Bibliography: 1958-1959 Publications in Comparative and International Education.* U.S. Office of Education, Division of International Education. Washington, U.S. Government Printing Office. 2 v., 1959, 111 p., 1960, 118 p.

Economic Development Institute. *Selected Readings and Source Material on Economic Development.* Washington, Economic Development Institute, International Bank for Reconstruction and Development, 1961. 66 p.

Hart, Donn Vorhis and Paul Meadows. *An Annotated Bibliography of Directed Social Change.* Prepared for the Pakistan Project [of] Syracuse University, Maxwell Graduate School of Citizenship and Public Affairs, Center for Overseas Operations. Syracuse, New York, 1961. 1 v. (unpaged)

Schleiffer, H. *Selective Bibliography on the Economic and Political Development of Indonesia.* Cambridge, Massachusetts Institute of Technology, Center for International Studies, 1955. 61 p.

Trager, F. N. *A Selected and Annotated Bibliography on Economic Development, 1953-1957, Part I.* Chicago, Economic Development and Cultural Change, v. 6, no. 4, July, 1958, p. 257-329.

U.S. Library of Congress, General Reference and Bibliography Division, African Section. *United States and Canadian Publications on Africa in 1960.* Washington, U.S. Government Printing Office, 1962. 98 p.

Viet, Jean. *International Cooperation and Programmes of Economic and Social Development. An Annotated Bibliography.* Paris, UNESCO, 1962. 107 p.

## 2. Books and Pamphlets

American Assembly. *The Representation of the United States Abroad. Background Papers Prepared for the Use of Participants and the Final Report of the Fifth American Assembly, May 3-6, 1956.* New York, The American Assembly, Graduate School of Business, Columbia University, 1956. 217 p.

Andrews, Stanley. *Technical Assistance Case Reports; Selected Projects in Nine Countries.* East Lansing, Michigan, Michigan State University, 1961.

Black, Eugene. *Tales of Two Continents: Africa and South America.* Athens, Georgia, University of Georgia Press, 1961. 36 p.

Carr, William George. *Only by Understanding: Education and International Organization.* Headline Series, No. 52, May-June, 1945. New York, Foreign Policy Association, 1945. 96 p.

Chamberlain, Lawrence H., and Richard C. Snyder. *American Foreign Policy.* New York, Rinehart and Company, Inc., 1948. 826 p. Chapter XV, "International Information and Foreign Policy," p. 372-398.

Conference of African States on the Development of Education in Africa, Addis Ababa, 1961. *Final Report.* United Nations Economic Commission for Africa, 1961. 127 p.

Conference on Extension Development Around the World, Washington, D.C., 1961. *Extension Development Around the World; Guidelines for Building Extension Organizations and Programs.* Washington, Federal Extension Service. U.S. Department of Agriculture, 1962. 30 p.

Daniels, Walter M., editor. *The Point Four Program.* New York, The
  H. W. Wilson Company, 1951. (*The Reference Shelf*, v. 23, no. 5).
  207 p. Bibliography, p. 189-207.
Eisenhower, Dwight D. *Toward a Common Goal. A Program for Economic
  Development.* An Address by President Eisenhower at the Colombo
  Plan Meeting, November 10, 1958. Washington, U.S. Government
  Printing Office, 1958. 14 p.
Erasmus, Charles J. *Man Takes Control. Cultural Development and Amer-
  ican Aid.* Minneapolis, University of Minnesota Press, 1961. 365 p.
Esman, Milton J. *Needed: An Education and Research Base to Support
  America's Expanded Commitments Overseas.* Pittsburgh, Pennsyl-
  vania, University of Pittsburgh Press, 1961. 46 p.
Food and Agriculture Organization of the United Nations. *Agreement for
  the Establishment on a Permanent Basis of a Latin-American Forest
  Research and Training Institute under the Auspices of the Food
  and Agriculture Organization of the United Nations.* Rome, November 20, 1959. London, H. M. Stationery Office, 1961. 44 p.
Food and Agriculture Organization of the United Nations. *Agreement for
  the Establishment of a Latin American Forest Research and Training Institute.* Rome, November 20, 1959. London, H. M. Stationery
  Office, 1960. 14 p.
———, *FAO's Role in Rural Welfare, Tenth Session,* Rome, 31 October
  1959. 114 p.
———, *The Agricultural Development of Peru, Report of a Mission Organized by the Food and Agriculture Organization of the United Na-
  tions and the International Bank for Reconstruction and
  Development at the Request of the Government of Peru.* Washing-
  ton, 1959. v. 1.
Frost, Raymond. *The Backward Society.* New York, St. Martin's Press,
  1961. 246 p.
Great Britain, Central Office of Information, Reference Division. *Britain's
  Contribution to Economic Development Overseas.* London, 1960.
  32 p. (No. RF.P. 4579).
Hazelwood, Arthur. *The Economics of "Under-Developed" Areas.* London,
  Oxford University Press. 1954. 84 p.
———, *The Economics of Underdeveloped Areas.* London, Oxford Uni-
  versity Press. 1959. 156 p.
Hickman, C. Addison. *World Economic Problems.* New York, Pitman Pub-
  lishing Corporation, 1947. 400 p.
Hoselitz, Bert F., editor. *The Progress of Underdeveloped Areas.* Chicago,
  The University of Chicago Press, 1952. 297 p.
Institute of International Education. *A Report to the President of the
  United States.* Washington, 1961. 15 p.
Institute of International Education, Committee on Educational Inter-

change Policy. *Educational Exchange in the Economic Development of Nations.* New York, 1961. 25 p.

*International Cooperation Workshop.* Washington, National Conference on International Economic and Social Development, 1958. 36 p. List of Organizations Represented, p. 35-36.

International Labour Office. *Report to the Government of Afghanistan on a Survey of Small-Scale Leather Industries in Afghanistan.* Geneva, 1959. 59 p.

——, *Report to the Government of Pakistan on a Productivity Survey Mission in the Jute Industry; December 1959-January 1960.* Geneva, 1960. 13 p.

——, *Report to the Government of Tanganyika on the Possibilities of Developing Industrial Co-operatives.* Geneva, 1961. 20 p.

Kandel, Isaac Leon. *Intellectual Cooperation: National and International.* New York, Teachers College, Columbia University, 1944. 78 p.

Kindleberger, C. P. *Economic Development.* New York, McGraw-Hill, 1958. 325 p.

Leibenstein, Harvey. *Economic Backwardness and Economic Growth.* New York, John Wiley and Sons, Inc., 1957. 295 p.

Mason, Edward S. *Economic Planning in Underdeveloped Areas.* New York, Fordham University Press, 1958. 87 p.

Meier, Gerald M. *Economic Development.* New York, John Wiley and Sons, Inc., 1957. 588 p. Part 3, "Accelerating Development in Poor Countries," p. 273-448.

Meyer, Adolph E. *The Development of Education in the Twentieth Century. New York,* Prentice-Hall, Inc., 1949. 609 p. "International Education," p. 569-587.

Mezerik, A. G., editor. *Economic Development Aids for Underdeveloped Countries; UN Sources; National and International Agencies; Financial and Technical Assistance; (with) Special Section on Africa.* New York, International Review Service, 1961. 108 p. (International Review Service. Analysis and Review of International Problems. v. 7, No. 63.)

McLaughlin, Kathleen. *The World's War on Want; How United Nations Members Share Skills and Resources through Technical Assistance.* New York, Oceana Publications, 1961. 80 p.

National Research Council. Ad Hoc Committee on Engineering for the Developing Countries. *Engineering for the Developing Countries, an Introductory Study.* Washington, National Academy of Sciences, National Research Council, 1961. 41 p. (National Research Council. Publication 947.)

Nehru, (His Excellency) Braj Kumar. *Foreign Aid from the Viewpoint of the Recipient Countries.* Washington, The Information Service of India, 1961. 21 p. Processed.

Nurkse, Ragnar. *Problems of Capital Formation in the Underdeveloped Countries.* New York, Oxford University Press, 1958. 163 p.

Okun, Bernard and Richard W. Richardson. *Studies in Economic Development Planning.* New York, Holt, Rinehart and Winston, 1961. 498 p.

Organization of American States. *Latin American Higher Education and Interamerican Cooperation; Report and Recommendations.* Washington, Pan American Union, 1961. 20 p.

Pentony, DeVere Edwin. *The Underdeveloped Lands; a Dilemma of the International Economy,* Compiled and Edited by DeVere E. Pentony with the Assistance of Morley Segal and Marilyn Derichs. San Francisco, H. Chandler, 1960. 196 p.

Pepelasis, Adamantios, Leon Mears and Irma Adelman. *Economic Development: Analysis and Case Studies.* New York, Harper & Brothers. 1961. 620 p.

Platt, William J. *Toward Strategies of Education.* Menlo Park, California, Stanford Research Institute, 1961. 37 p.

Robinson, E. A. G., editor. *Economic Consequences of the Size of Nations.* New York, St. Martin's Press, Inc., 1960. 447 p. Chapter 8, The Problems of Developing Countries.

Santa Cruz, Herman. *FAO's Role in Rural Welfare.* Rome, Food and Agriculture Organization of the United Nations, 1959. 177 p.

Scott, John. *Democracy Is Not Enough: A Personal Survey of the Hungry World.* New York, Harcourt, Brace and World. 1960. 177 p.

Shannon, Lyle W. *Underdeveloped Areas.* New York, Harper & Brothers, 1957. 476 p.

Sharp, Walter R., and Grayson Kirk. *Contemporary International Politics.* New York, Farrar and Rinehart, Inc., 1944. 876 p.

*Significant Issues in Economic Aid to Newly Developing Countries.* Menlo Park, California, International Industrial Development Center, 1960. (Staff paper.) 75 p. Bibliography, p. 71-75.

Staley, Eugene. *The Future of Underdeveloped Countries.* New York, Harper & Brothers, 1954. 410 p.

Stoker, Spencer. *The Schools and International Understanding.* Chapel Hill, North Carolina, The University of North Carolina Press, 1933. 243 p.

Sufi, M. H. and others. *A Report on Agricultural Extension Work in the U.S.A. and Reorganization of Extension Services in Pakistan.* Karachi, Printed by the Assistant Manager, Government of Pakistan Press, 1952. 39 p.

*Technical Assistance in Brief. Programs of United Nations and Specialized Agencies.* New York, United Nations, 1958. 12 p.

*Technical Cooperation: The Dramatic Story of Helping Others to Help Themselves.* U.S. International Cooperation Administration. Washington, U.S. Government Printing Office, 1959. 59 p. (U.S. Department of State Publication No. 6815.)

United Nations. Department of Public Information. *Helping Economic Development in Asia and the Far East; the Work of ECAFE.* New York, United Nations Office of Public Information, 1960. 52 p.

——, *Helping Southeast Asia to Help Itself.* New York, United Nations, 1957. 60 p. Selected Bibliography, p. 58-60.

——, *Technical Assistance: What? How? Why?* New York, United Nations, 1957. 64 p. Suggested Reading List, p. 60-64.

——, *United Nations Aid to Africa.* New York, United Nations, 1962. 15 p.

United Nations Economic Commission for Asia and the Far East, Group of Experts on Programming Techniques. *Formulating Industrial Development Programs, with Special Reference to Asia and the Far East.* Bangkok, United Nations Economic Commission for Asia and the Far East, 1961. 137 p.

United Nations, Educational, Scientific and Cultural Organization. *Asia, Arab States, Africa. Education and Progress.* Paris, 1961. 63 p.

U.S. Department of State, Division of International Organization Affairs. *International Organizations in Which the United States Participates.* Washington, U.S. Government Printing Office. 1946. 322 p.

U.S. Department of State. External Research Division. *Research on Underdevelopment; Assessment and Inventory of Research on Economic, Social and Political Problems of Underdeveloped Areas.* Washington, 1960. 1 v. (various pagings).

U.S. Information Agency. Near East Foundation. Economic Report No. 2076. February 4, 1955. 9 p. Processed.

U.S. International Cooperation Administration. *Technical Cooperation in Education.* Washington, U.S. Government Printing Office, 1960. 31 p. (U.S. Department of State Publication No. 7024. Economic Cooperation Series 58.)

——, *Technical Cooperation in Industry.* Washington, U.S. Government Printing Office, 1960. 23 p. (U.S. Department of State Publication No. 7023. Economic Cooperation Series 57.)

U.S. International Cooperation Administration, Office of Public Reports. *Technical Cooperation.* Washington, U.S. Government Printing Office, 1957. 38 p.

Wilson, Howard E. *United States National Commission for UNESCO.* New York, The Macmillan Company, 1948. 96 p.

——, *Universities and World Affairs.* New York, Carnegie Endowment for International Peace, 1951. 88 p.

Wright, Quincy, editor. *A Foreign Policy for the United States.* Chicago, The University of Chicago Press, 1947. 405 p.

APPENDIX : 191

Zolotas, Xenophon. *Economic Development and Technical Education.* Athens, 1960. 60 p.

**3. Articles in Periodicals**

Adiseshiah, M. S. "Technical Assistance in Asia." London, *Eastern World,* v. XIV, No. 5, May, 1960, p. 16-19.

"Aid to Africa: United Nations Interest, Effort Intensified." New York, *United Nations Review,* v. 8, September, 1961, p. 28-29.

Benham, F. C. "Education and Economic Development in the Underdeveloped Countries." London, *International Affairs,* v. 35, No. 2, April, 1959, p. 181-187.

Berg, Sherwood O. and Arthur T. Mosher. "International Opportunities for American Land-Grant Universities." Menasha, Wisconsin, *Journal of Farm Economics,* v. 43, December, 1961, p. 1056-1067.

Caldwell, Oliver J. "Education Provides a New Approach to Diplomacy." Chicago, *The Nation's Schools,* v. 53, No. 2, February, 1954, p. 43-47.

Cheema, Amrik Singh. "In India: Working Together for a Better Living." Washington, *Extension Service Review,* v. 29, December, 1958, p. 243, 246.

"Employment Objectives in Economic Development." Geneva, *International Labour Review,* v. 84, November, 1961, p. 394-411.

Evans, T. H. "A New Approach: The Regional School." London, *Overseas,* v. 1, April, 1962, p. 20-24.

Ezekiel, Mordecai. "Ten Years of FAO Statistics and Economics Training Centers." Menasha, Wisconsin, *Journal of Farm Economics,* v. 39, May, 1957, p. 221-234.

v Furrer-Haimendorf, Christoph. "The West in the 'Underdeveloped' Countries." Zurich, Switzerland, *Swiss Review of World Affairs,* v. 8, December, 1958, p. 16-18.

Glick, Philip M. "The Choice of Instruments for Technical Cooperation." Philadelphia, *Annals of the American Academy of Political and Social Science,* v. 323, May, 1959, p. 59-67.

Graham, F. P. "Work and Hopes of the United Nations in the Atomic Age." Chicago, *College and University,* v. 31, no. 4, 1956, p. 417-22.

Grissom, John W. "A Decade of Technical Assistance." Washington, U.S. Department of Health, Education and Welfare, Office of Education, *School Life,* v. 44, May, 1962, p. 15-18.

Hale, Alan. "Revolution in Technical Aid." London, *New Commonwealth,* v. 40, May, 1962, p. 280-282.

Hanna, Paul R. "Education as an Economic and Social Instrument in the Newly Developing Nations." Bloomington, Indiana, *Phi Delta Kappan,* v. 43, May, 1962, p. 354-356.

Hull, W. J. "Growing Pains of International Technical Co-operation."

Geneva, *International Labour Review*, v. 1, October, 1961, p. 223-245.

"International Technical Cooperation—2, Sources of Aid Other Than From the United Kingdom." London, *Journal of Local Administration Overseas*, v. 1, April, 1962, p. 112-123.

Kandel, I. L. "Comparative Education and Underdeveloped Countries." New York, *Comparative Education Review*, v. 4, February, 1961, p. 130-135.

Kaul, P. M. "Role of WHO in the Congo." Nashville, Tennessee, *Journal of the American Medical Women's Association*, v. 16, April, 1961, p. 287-289.

Kent, George. "Medical Samaritans on Safari." Pleasantville, New York, *Reader's Digest*, v. 79, October, 1961, p. 172-73, 175-76, 179-80.

Mboya, Tom. "African Higher Education; A Challenge to America." Boston, Massachusetts, *Atlantic Monthly*, v. 208, July, 1961, p. 23-26.

Rens, Jef. "The Andean Programme." Geneva, *International Labour Review*, v. 84, December, 1961, p. 423-461.

————, "The ILO and International Technical Co-operation." Geneva, *International Labour Review*, v. 83, May, 1961, p. 413-415.

Roucche, Earl. "Experts on Call." Washington, *Americas*, v. 13, June, 1961, p. 14-15.

Ruffner, R. W. "American Educational Aid for National Development." New York, *Teachers College Record*, v. 62, February, 1961, p. 348-355.

Rusk, D. "Education: Key to National Development." New York, Institute of International Education, *Overseas*, v. 1, September, 1961, p. 6-7.

Smuckler, Ralph H. "Michigan State University Project at Vietnam." New York, Institute of International Education, *IIE News Bulletin*, v. 35, May, 1960, p. 2-6.

"Special Fund's New Projects Approved for Thirty-Six Low-Income Countries." New York, *United Nations Review*, v. 8, July, 1961, p. 14-17.

Stevenson, Adlai E. "Approaching the Problem of African Development." Washington, *Department of State Bulletin*, v. 44, April 10, 1961, p. 534-537.

Stevenson, Charles. "Bright Spot on the Dark Continent." Pleasantville, New York, *Reader's Digest*, v. 77, July, 1960, 118-123.

Tead, O. "What Are America's Purposes?" Tiffin, Ohio, *Educational Forum*, v. 25, March, 1961, p. 317-23.

"Ten Years of Multilateral Skill-Sharing." New York, *United Nations Review*, July, 1959, p. 28-34.

"The Expanded Program of Technical Assistance." New York, *United Nations Review*, v. 8, February, 1960, p. 46-48.

Tretyakov, P. "Soviet Technical Assistance to Underdeveloped Countries."

Moscow, *International Affairs,* v. 1960, No. 2, February, 1960, p. 46-50.

Triantis, Stephen G. "Backward Lands—the Other Front." Toronto, Canada, Canadian Institute of International Affairs, *Behind the Headlines,* v. XII, No. 2, February, 1952, 16 p.

"U.S. Medicine Abroad." Chicago, *Today's Health,* v. 39, No. 9, September, 1961, p. 23-27.

"What Is Economic Development? III. How Governments Can Help to Promote Economic Development." New York, *United Nations Review,* v. 5, No. 10, April, 1959, p. 21-27. Recruitment and Training, p. 23.

Zuckerman, Sir Solly. "Scientific and Technical Aid for Africa." Johannesburg, South Africa, *Optima,* v. 10, March, 1960, p. 4-9.

# INDEX

Aasland, Lasse, 146
Adair, Charles W., 156
Ahmed, Zahiruddin, 24-27, 40, 47, 67,
  91, 153
Algeria, trade union cooperation in,
  99
Alianza Corps, creation of, 147
Altarelli, Angelo, 152
Amaro de Brito, Flavio, 63, 91, 150
American Council of Voluntary Agen-
  cies for Foreign Service, 156
American Council on Education, 156
American Telephone and Telegraph,
  107
Andresen, Rudolf K., 124, 153
Area Redevelopment Act, U.S. (1961),
  58
Arellano, Oscar, 157
Argentina,
  economic growth in, 18
  volunteer service program of, 147
Army as training area, 73-74
Arnesen, Arne, 153
Asian Productivity Organization (APO),
  155
Association of Voluntary Builders, 126
Atthakor, Nai Boonchana, 72, 154
Australia, delegate from, 149
Austria,
  delegates from, 149

skill development on the job in, 77,
  82-83
Austrian Federation of Trade Unions,
  99
Avriel, Ehud, 151

Bar-on, Hanan, 151
Basdevant, Jean, 64-65, 151
Belgium,
  delegates from, 149
  volunteer service program of, 126
Ben Ammar, Mondher, 64, 154
Benjenk, Munir, 156
Bernick, Paul, 156
Bentancur Cuartas, Belisario, 117, 118,
  150
Bielka-Karltreu, Erich, 82, 149
Bjerkholt, Aase, 124, 153
Bjornberg, Arne, 154
Bode, Karl F., 157
Bolin, Bertil, 154
Bolivia,
  delegates from, 149
  training manpower in, 69
Bourguiba, Habib, Jr., 154
Brasseur, Maurice, 126, 149
Braude, Max, 157
Brazil,
  delegate from, 150
  economic growth in, 18

## About the Editors

FRANCIS W. GODWIN has worked in the field of overseas economic development for twenty-two years. Since 1950, he has served as a consultant to the World Bank, various foreign governments, U.S. agencies and the United Nations. More than half these years he has lived and worked in the developing areas of the world. He is currently planning consultant to the Peace Corps, and was an officer of the San Juan Conference Secretariat.

Known mainly as a specialist on industrialization of the developing countries, he has long emphasized the primary development of human resources and domestic technology as a precondition for the economic growth process. Under World Bank auspices, he helped to draw up the five-year plans of half a dozen growing nations, and he prepared the first over-all study of the technological needs of Latin America for the initial meeting of the United Nations ECLA. In 1947, mobilizing a staff of Mexican technologists, he organized the first local research institute to help the young industries in an emerging country, a pattern later followed in Ceylon (where he also acted as director) and numerous other countries.

Mr. Godwin is co-author or editor of six books on development, the last four of which are World Bank studies published by Johns Hopkins Press, and he has also published many articles on scientific matters, training and research organization in U.S. and foreign periodicals.

RICHARD N. GOODWIN, Secretary General of the International Peace Corps Secretariat which grew out of the San Juan Conference, participated in the conference as a member of the United States Delegation.

A 1953 graduate of Tufts, he entered Harvard Law School, where, after a two-year interruption in the Army, he earned his LL.B. in 1958, summa cum laude, and was president of the Harvard *Law Review*.

Until the spring of 1959, he served as law clerk for Justice Felix Frankfurter, then was appointed Special Counsel for the House Subcommittee on Legislative Oversight.

In 1961, Mr. Goodwin joined the White House staff as Assistant Special Counsel to the President on Latin American matters, then served as Deputy Assistant Secretary of State until January, 1963, when he assumed his present duties as head of the new International Secretariat.

**WILLIAM F. HADDAD**, presently Associate Director of the U.S. Peace Corps, was Secretary General of the San Juan Conference.

After service as an officer in the Merchant Marine, he received his B.A. from Columbia College, and did graduate work at both Columbia and Georgetown University. He then entered the government and served on the Senate Judiciary Committee, the Senate Subcommittee on Juvenile Delinquency, and as special assistant to Senator Kefauver on his world tours.

Subsequently, as a New York *Post* reporter, specializing in municipal affairs, he helped to found the New York City reform movement. His exposés resulted in the summoning of a dozen grand juries and the solution of at least one murder, and won for him many distinguished journalism awards.

In 1960, he became special assistant to Robert Kennedy, then moved to the newly formed Peace Corps as special assistant to Sargent Shriver. In his present post, he directs the Corps' constant objective field evaluation of its own work, and is in charge of both the agency's planning and Special Projects Division.